SECOND EDITION 2

HIGHER History

ourse notes book 2

John A Kerr

01/150810

ISBN 978-1-84372-698-2

Published by
Leckie & Leckie
an imprint of HarperCollins*Publishers*
Westerhill Road, Bishopbriggs, Glasgow G64 2QT|
Tel: 0844 576 8126 Fax: 0844 576 8131
leckieandleckie@harpercollins.co.uk www.leckieandleckie.co.uk

Special thanks to
Helen Bleck (proofreading),
Roda Morrison (copy-edit),
Integra-India (creative packaging)

A CIP Catalogue record for this book is available from the British Library.

The cover image shows a statue commemorating the declaration of Arbroath, signed in 1320.

The content and the style of questions contained in paper 2 of the Higher History exam have changed for the 2011 and later exams. Paper 2 is now based on a study of one Scottish History topic.

This book contains what you need to know about three popular Scottish History topics.

1. The Scottish Wars of Independence, 1286–1328
2. The Treaty of Union, 1689–1740
3. The Impact of the Great War on Scotland, 1914–1928.

In your Higher History course you will learn about **one** topic only. If you are learning about any one of the topics listed above then this book is for you!

This book does 2 things:

1. It gives all the information needed to answer successfully the questions asked about on your Scottish History topic.
2. It provides advice and guidance about how your answers will be marked and how your answers should be constructed.

The book is divided into 3 parts.

Part 1 is called *Practise Your Skills*.

You don't have to read this first but it will be useful to you when you write your own answers. The section explains how each of the types of question will be worded, what they will ask about and how your answers will be marked.

Part 2 and 3 are combined.

Part 2 gives all the content necessary for the course, written in easy to understand sections. At the end of each topic, the relevant piece of part 3 gives you examples of the different types of questions. You will also find advice on how to structure your answers. There are also examples of good and not so good answers for you to mark, using the SQA rules.

Leckie & Leckie also produce more books to help you be successful in Higher History.

- *Higher History Course Notes Book 1* focuses on paper 1. It provides the content you need and also advice on how to structure essays that will gain you top marks!
- *Higher History Grade Booster* gives practical advice on the entire Higher History exam including how to be successful in the extended essay.
- *Practice Papers for SQA exams – Higher History* gives you all you need to know about what the real exam will look like, the sorts of questions asked and advice on how to answer the questions.

All these books are written by John A Kerr, a very experienced Higher History exam setter and marker. John Kerr is also the author of many textbooks for Standard Grade, Intermediate 1 and 2 and Higher History.

For Higher History Paper 2 you will study in depth one unit about Scottish History. You will be asked four questions about your chosen unit. Each question will be of a different type.

- There will be a 'How useful …'/source evaluation question worth 5 marks.
- There will be a comparison question worth 5 marks.
- There will be a 'How far …' question worth 10 marks.
- There will be a 'How fully …' question worth 10 marks.

These types of question will not always appear in the same order but they **will** always be in your exam paper.

Your chosen study unit is divided into four main sections called 'Issues'. In your exam, each issue will have one question linked to it. One of the four types of questions will be used to find out what you know about each issue. In total you will be asked four questions about your chosen study unit.

After each main section in this book you will find a 'Practise your skills' section. These sections give you practice and advice in answering the different types of question.

Each 'Practise your skills' task provides:

- a source (or sources for comparison)
- where the source comes from (its provenance)
- a question
- advice on how to answer the question
- information about how answers to questions are marked.

Your challenge is to write answers that are structured well and which follow the advice in the mark schemes about what a good answer needs to get top marks.

Top Tip

Work with a friend. Exchange answers and use the mark scheme to mark their work. This will help you in four ways.

1. By using the mark scheme, you will learn the rules about why marks are given.
2. You will need to justify and explain the marks you give to your friend so you will need to understand clearly why marks are awarded. Once you understand the rules, you can structure your answers more carefully so that you give a marker what he or she is looking for.
3. You may not like the mark your friend or teacher gives you but you will know **why** you got the mark and **how** you can improve future answers.
4. By doing this task you are **reinforcing your understanding** of how and why marks are given.

The 'How useful…' question

This is a source evaluation question and is worth 5 marks.

This question will always ask, 'How useful is the source as evidence of …'
You will get **up to** 2 marks for writing about the source's origin and its purpose. For 2 marks you will be expected to explain why the origin and purpose of the source is important to judging how useful it is.

You will get **up to** 2 marks for explaining why the parts of the source you have selected are relevant and helpful when judging how useful the source is. That means you do **not** get 2 marks just for quoting from the source.

You will get **up to** 2 marks for using **new** detailed knowledge, so long as it helps to answer the question. Try to include at least three different pieces of new detailed knowledge.

Top Tip

Make sure you have answered the question. In this case you **must** decide how **useful** the source is as historical evidence and you **must** make this assessment clear in your answer.

The Comparison question

The easy way to spot a comparison question is that it is the only question that will refer to **two** sources in the question. The question might not contain the word 'compare': it may ask something like 'To what extent does Source A agree with Source B about ...'

What do you have to do?

Firstly, you must make **an overall comparison**: you will get up to 2 marks for stating the main ideas or points of view in the two sources.
Secondly, there will always be four direct comparison points within the sources. Aim to find them all. You can get up to 4 marks for identifying the points of comparison **and** for using your own knowledge to explain all the comparison points in the source.

The 'How far...' question

The syllabus for this course is divided into 4 main issues: each issue is divided into separate parts called descriptors. A 'How far ...' question is based around one of those descriptors and wants to find out how much you know on that subject.
Usually the question will contain phrases such as 'How far does Source C show reasons for ...' or 'To what extent does Source A explain why ...'
The 'How far ...' question is worth 10 marks.

What do you have to do?

Firstly, you must choose relevant information from the source that helps to answer the question. Remember to explain how your source selections are relevant to the question. You can get up to 4 marks for doing that.
Secondly, you can get up to 7 marks for including as much accurate and relevant information from your own knowledge as you can.

Top Tip

The secret of success in **all** the questions apart from the comparison question is to write a **balanced** answer.
Use the word '**partly**'! By saying that a source explains something partly, you have the opportunity to use your own knowledge. Firstly, explain what the points you have selected from the source mean. Secondly, include your recalled knowledge to explain points that the source does not mention yet are relevant to your answer.

The 'How fully...' question

This question asks about one of the four main issues within your special study syllabus.
The 'How fully...' question is worth 10 marks and is similar in the way it is answered to the 'How far...' question. The difference is that while the 'How far...' question asks about one part of an issue, the 'How fully...' question asks about a whole issue.

What do you have to do?

Firstly, you must use the source provided.
You can get up to 4 marks for choosing relevant information in the source. Remember to explain how your source quotes are relevant to the question. Don't just list quotes!

Secondly, you must include your own accurate and relevant knowledge.
You can get up to 7 marks for including as much accurate and relevant information from your own knowledge as you can. The sources will never tell the full story so you are expected to use recall to develop your answer further.

The Wars of Independence, 1286–1328

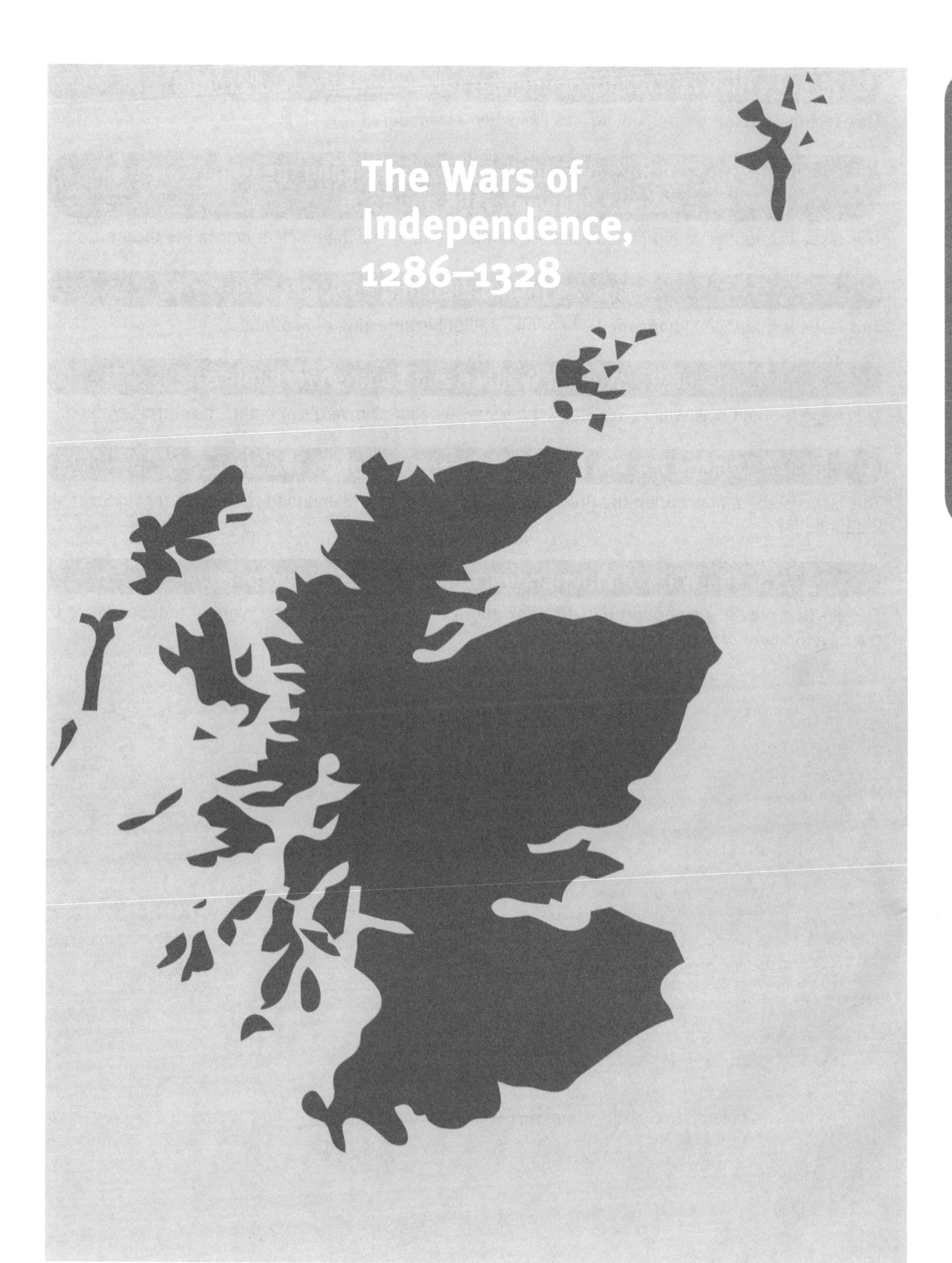

The Wars of Independence, 1286–1328: the background

This section is about what Scotland was like when Alexander III was king.

Issue 1 – Scotland, the succession problem and the Great Cause between 1286 and 1296

This issue is about what happened when Alexander III died, leaving no clear heir to the throne.

Issue 2 – John Balliol and Edward I

This issue is about what happened when John Balliol became king of Scotland.

Issue 3 – William Wallace and Scottish resistance

This issue is about how William Wallace led resistance against Edward's attempts to control Scotland.

Issue 4 – The rise and triumph of Robert the Bruce

This issue is about how Robert the Bruce became king of Scotland and then went on to regain Scottish independence.

The Wars of Independence, 1286–1328: a perspective

This section provides an opportunity to think about the significance of the Wars of Independence in the development of Scottish identity.

The Wars of Independence, 1286–1328: the background

This section is about what Scotland was like when Alexander III was king.

To cover the syllabus you should know about the following:

- Why the reign of Alexander III (1249–86) was called a Golden Age for Scotland.
- How Alexander increased his control over Scotland during his reign.
- Relations between Scotland and England during the reign of Alexander III.

Seal of Alexander III

Why was the death of Alexander III such a turning point in Scottish history?

The roots of the Wars of Independence lay in the sudden death of King Alexander III of Scotland. Without any clear successor to the throne, Scotland was left in a state of confusion. Would Scotland really be ruled by his granddaughter, a girl less than ten years old? Would Scotland be ripped apart by powerful nobles, all wanting to become king? Would King Edward of England try to take away Scotland's independence and absorb the nation of Scotland into England?

All these problems and questions arose after the death of Alexander III. In the years that followed, many Scots looked back on the reign of Alexander III as the 'good old days' when Scotland had a 'Golden Age' and everything was good.

Was there really a Golden Age under Alexander III?

A short verse written in the 13th century is often quoted as evidence that Scotland had a Golden Age under Alexander III. It reads,

> When Alexander our King was dead,
> That Scotland led in love and le,
> Away was wealth of ale and bread,
> Of wine and wax, of game and glee.
> Our gold was changed into lead.
> Christ born into virginity,
> Succour Scotland and remedy
> Which placèd is in perplexity. (Scotland is in trouble. Please help it.)

Essentially this poem is saying that Alexander was a popular king and led Scotland well. When he died, so did the good times, and hardship followed. However, is that a fair and accurate comment? Given the problems that Scotland faced during the Wars of Independence, is it not the case that anyone living through such difficult times would look back on the past with nostalgia and think of earlier times as the 'good old days'?

Royal authority under Alexander III

How did Alexander III increase his authority?

Under Alexander more people in the land we now call Scotland accepted the authority of the king. Alexander's law officers, called Royal Sheriffs, spread royal law and order across the land and Scotland became a more peaceful and prosperous place. As a result, people would certainly have felt safer going about their business.

Much of the present-day area now known as Scotland became established under Alexander III. Even before he became king, the Treaty of York in 1237 had settled the border between Scotland and England on a line very similar to where it is today. In 1263 the Scots won a victory over the Viking rulers of the Western Isles and, as a result of the Treaty of Perth in 1266, the Scottish king gained authority over much of the west of Scotland and the Isle of Man. (At this time Shetland and Orkney were still under the control of the king of Norway.)

Alexander also created a more modern system of law and order that made his own position as king more powerful. Older systems of law and order, especially in the western parts of Scotland (known as the Celtic area), were broken down. Alexander replaced older systems of law and authority with the more modern feudal system. In a feudal state the king owned all land. The king 'gave' parts of that land to important nobles in exchange for promises of support and loyalty (fealty). At a special ceremony the lords receiving the land from the king did homage for the land and made binding promises of support. If the nobles broke their promises of loyalty, then they would lose their land. Under the feudal system the king increased his authority by making it clear to the nobles that it was in their best interests to stay loyal to the king.

How did the economy of Scotland grow under Alexander?

Under Alexander, Scotland was an exporter of raw materials such as wool, hides, timber and fish and traded a great deal with northern European ports and with Ireland. Berwick upon Tweed was Scotland's most important money-making port. Aberdeen, Ayr, Glasgow and Inverness also played important parts in the economy.

Coins from Alexander III's reign

As the economy grew so did the spread of coins, each with the image of the king on it. The acceptance of coins not only spread the acceptance of the king's authority, it also represented the spread of trust and stability in the system of trade that was developing around trading centres and market days in burgh towns and villages. Without confidence in law and order, few merchants would have risked carrying their goods long distances to open markets.

Scotland's relationship with England

How did Scotland get on with England under Alexander III?

The answer is that Scotland and England got on very well while Alexander III was king. Alexander III was King Edward of England's brother-in-law. Old arguments about where the border lay between Scotland and England had been sorted out and both nations saw advantages in the trade that was growing between them. However, by the 1270s, the problem of overlordship still rumbled on.

What was the 'overlord' argument about?

For a long time Scottish kings had made varying claims over ruling large parts of northern England. On the other side of the argument, English kings persistently claimed that they were more important than Scottish kings. This claim revolved around the issue of overlordship.

The problem lay in that many Scottish nobles – and even the Scottish king – possessed land in England. They had sworn loyalty for their English land to the English king, so the question arose: who was the more important king? Could the swearing of loyalty mean that the English king had authority – or overlordship – over the Scottish king?

The issue came to a head when Edward I of England insisted that Alexander III do homage not only for the lands that Alexander held in England but **also** for the kingdom of Scotland. To do homage meant to make promises of loyalty to the overlord and promise to obey him in everything. Alexander said he would do homage for the land he held in England but refused to do homage for any lands in Scotland. If Alexander had done homage for his Scottish lands then he would have been accepting that Edward was overlord of Scotland!

During the reign of Alexander III this issue of overlordship was not resolved but was just 'brushed under the carpet'. By the 1280s it seemed that relations between Scotland and England were as stable as they had ever been. Then King Alexander died, and Scotland's Golden Age died with him.

Issue 1 – Scotland, the succession problem and the Great Cause between 1286 and 1296

This issue is about what happened when Alexander III died, leaving no clear heir to the throne.

To cover the syllabus you should know about the following:

- Why there was no clear heir to the throne after the death of Margaret, Maid of Norway.
- What Scotland did to maintain its independence.
- Why Edward I of England became involved in the choice of Scotland's next king.
- What is meant by the Great Cause, and how Edward used it to his advantage.

Edward I

The succession problem

Why was Alexander's death such a disaster for Scotland?

Quite simply, Alexander III had no living relative ready to become Scotland's next king or queen. It was vital for kings at this time to have an heir old enough and strong enough to take over power but Alexander's wife, son and daughter had all died. When Alexander fell to his death one stormy night as he travelled to be with his new bride Yolande, Scotland faced a serious problem.

Although Alexander's royal authority had been strong there were ambitious, powerful nobles who saw the empty throne as an opportunity to increase their power. The two strongest families were the Bruce and the Balliol/Comyn families. Both sides built up their armies and it looked like Scotland would face civil war. Then a compromise was reached, which involved a young Norwegian girl, the Maid of Norway.

How did the Maid of Norway become a central figure in Scotland's future after 1286?

The Treaty of Perth was a peace treaty between Norway and Scotland agreed in 1266. The peace was sealed with the marriage of Alexander's daughter to the king of Norway. That daughter was now dead, but Alexander's granddaughter, Margaret, still lived. When Alexander died, his granddaughter was only about four years old. Clearly, she could not rule Scotland. However, two years earlier, in 1284, Alexander had made the nobles promise to accept Margaret as queen if the unthinkable happened and he died suddenly with no other heirs. Now the unthinkable was reality. Would the nobles keep their promise?

Who were the Guardians of Scotland?

The Guardians were a group of six nobles, entrusted to rule Scotland until Margaret was old enough to do so herself. The Guardians were also chosen to represent different powerful groups in Scottish society. Two were bishops, two were barons and the remaining two were earls.

Together, the Guardians formed part of what later historians came to call the Community of the Realm. The Community of the Realm is an important concept to understand. It showed that different individuals were prepared to work together for the good of the kingdom (the realm). By working as a Community, they were looking to the good of the nation rather than their individual gain. Such ideas were not common in Europe at this time; hence the importance of the Community of the Realm as an significant political development in medieval society.

The Guardians hoped they could guide and protect Margaret until she was old enough to rule Scotland on her own. Until then, having a young girl as queen was a big risk for Scotland.

Whoever helped her to make decisions as a child queen would have to be trusted to work for the benefit of Scotland and not simply for himself. As a young girl, Margaret would be unable to lead the Scottish army into battle so who would become the military leader and command the respect of Scotland's army? Also, as queen of Scotland, Margaret would inevitably become the focus of ambitious men who would try to marry her and in that way gain control over Scotland. That is exactly what seemed to be happening when Edward of England suggested a marriage between his son and Margaret.

In what ways did the Treaty of Birgham seem to protect Scotland's interests?

King Edward of England was the young Margaret's grand-uncle. Naturally, he was interested in her wellbeing but he also saw a way of expanding his influence over Scotland. He suggested a marriage between the young Margaret and his own son, who was then only ten years old. Both sides seemed happy and the Treaty of Birgham signed in 1290 agreed that a marriage would take place between Margaret and young Prince Edward.

The positive results of a marriage would be that the threat of civil war in Scotland would vanish and the simmering issue of overlordship and boundary disputes would be resolved. On the other hand, any child of the marriage would become ruler of both England and Scotland. That, however, had been common political practice in Europe for centuries as a way of ensuring peace between countries.

The Guardians were well aware that they might be giving away Scotland's independence by agreeing to the marriage, so they included several important sections designed to protect Scotland's freedoms. The Guardians intended the Treaty of Birgham to keep Scotland separate and free from control by England.

In detail, the treaty stated that the Scottish Church would remain free from interference from England, Scottish nobles who held land from the king of Scotland would only do homage to the king of Scotland and no one accused of a crime in Scotland would have their crime tried under English law. Finally, Scots would only be taxed to pay for Scottish needs and the taxes collected in Scotland would not be used by England for its needs.

The Guardians were undoubtedly suspicious of Edward's motives, but they seemed satisfied with the conditions laid down at Birgham.

Then Margaret died in 1290 and it all fell apart. The Treaty of Birgham was now useless. Scotland faced the prospect of civil war and the worry about what Edward of England would do next.

How real was the threat of civil war in Scotland?

When news of Margaret's death spread across Scotland, there was a very real danger of civil war. The death of the Maid of Norway created a political vacuum and a second disaster for Scotland within ten years.

Now there really was no-one who had an automatic right to rule Scotland and it seemed likely that, to use a phase from the 20th century, power would come from the barrel of a gun – or, in medieval terms, from the blade of a sharp sword.

Rival groups began to show their power. It was clear that the Bruce family were raising forces in south-west Scotland and that Comyn's allies were doing likewise in the north. The evidence of this comes from a letter sent by William Fraser, Bishop of St Andrews, who wrote to King Edward asking him to come to the Scottish border to maintain peace. Fraser described how powerful families in Scotland were raising armies to fight for the right to be king. Fraser continued by saying how there was a widespread fear of war and slaughter if the succession issue was not settled peacefully. It was clear that only King Edward had the power and strength to make the Scottish nobility stop the rush to civil war.

To avoid this, the Guardians asked Edward of England to decide who should be next ruler of Scotland. So began the period of time that came to be known as the Great Cause.

The Great Cause

What was the Great Cause?

The Great Cause is the name given to the time when Edward sat in judgement over the question of who should be next king of Scotland. Although there were thirteen competitors (as the claimants were called) only three really mattered – John Hastings, Robert Bruce (the grandfather of Robert I [the Bruce]) and John Balliol (a close ally of the Comyns).

How did Edward use the Great Cause to his advantage?

Edward did indeed go to the Scottish border, but not quite as the peacemaker Fraser had intended. The Guardians of Scotland rode to meet Edward but right away Edward started playing political games.

The Guardians expected Edward to cross the River Tweed and meet them on Scottish soil. Instead, Edward played his hand carefully.

First of all, Edward insisted the Scots cross the Tweed and come to him. Secondly, Edward arrived with a large army and based himself at Norham Castle, just over the Tweed on the English side. The threat was clear to the Scots. Thirdly, Edward insisted the Scots recognise him as their overlord. As Edward argued, how else could he give the right to rule Scotland to someone else if he did not already own it first?

The Scots tried to delay making an answer. Eventually they claimed that without a king of their own they could not reach a decision about the ownership of the land of Scotland. However, Edward was not prepared to wait. He had already asked all English monasteries (where official records were kept) to search for any documents supporting his claim to overlordship. Edward had also begun to build up a large army to enforce his will over Scotland if necessary. It was clear that Edward's ambitions towards Scotland had changed, at least in terms of the speed with which he wanted to assert his influence.

What was the Award of Norham?

The Award of Norham is the name given to the acceptance of Edward's overlordship by the claimants to the throne of Scotland. Edward had successfully outmanoeuvred, not only the Guardians, but also all the claimants to the throne. If they wished to be considered for the title of king, each claimant would have to accept Edward as his superior. If they did not, then their claim would be rejected.

The claimants had no choice but to accept Edward as judge and agreed that he should have possession of the lands of Scotland, on the condition that when the case was settled, Edward would restore the realm of Scotland to the successful candidate. The date was 3 June 1291. Edward was now the legal owner of Scotland.

Once the agreement about temporary overlordship was reached 104 'auditors' (forty chosen by Balliol, forty by Bruce and twenty-four by Edward) heard and discussed the evidence. They then reported directly to Edward so that he could reach his decision.

Why did Edward choose Balliol?

Although all the claimants to the throne were in some way related to the royal line of Scotland, none had a clear and close connection.

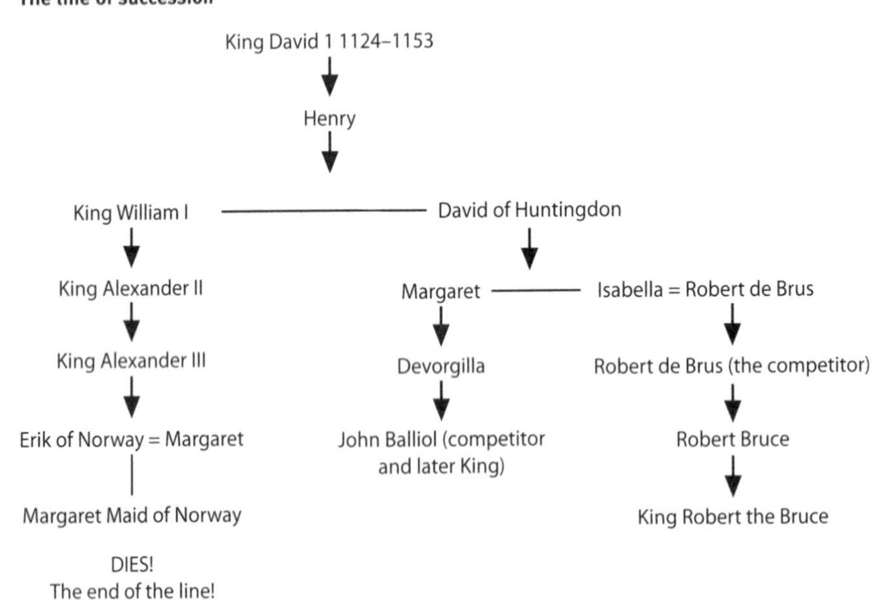

When the royal line died with the Maid of Norway, the nearest royal relative had to be found. The royal link went back to David of Huntingdon, the brother of King William. David of Huntingdon had two daughters:

- His first daughter was Margaret. She had a daughter called Devorgilla, and Devorgilla was the mother of John Balliol.
- His second daughter was Isabella. She had a son called Robert de Brus – the competitor.

John Balliol was three generations away from David of Huntingdon, while Robert de Brus was only two generations away from David. However, Edward chose John Balliol because he was descended from David's first daughter, according to the law of primogeniture.

The first competitor, John Hastings, argued that Scotland should be divided between the claimants. Neither the other claimants nor Edward would agree to that so Hastings' claim was quickly rejected. That left Robert Bruce and John Balliol.

Robert Bruce was nearly eighty. He claimed he was nearest by a generation to the royal line of Scotland. On the other hand, John Balliol was the grandson of the first-born child in the branch of the family tree that Bruce was also using to justify his claim. Bruce was the son of the second-born child. Under the law of primogeniture (the law that states inheritance of titles or property passes through the first-born child) Balliol was clearly the correct legal choice and on 17 November 1292 Edward announced that Balliol would be the next king of Scotland.

Issue 2 – John Balliol and Edward I

This issue is about what happened when John Balliol became king of Scotland.

To cover the syllabus you should know about the following:

- Whether John was a good king or not.
- How Edward tried to overrule Balliol and assert his overlordship.
- Why Scotland and England went to war.
- How Edward defeated Scotland and then tried to take away its identity as a free and independent nation.

The rule of John Balliol

How did Edward start to assert his authority over Balliol?

Almost as soon as Edward announced his decision (on 17 November 1292) that John Balliol should be king of Scotland, Edward put pressure on Balliol and began to undermine his authority in Scotland.

Balliol was in a difficult position. Edward insisted that Balliol pay homage and swear fealty to him. That meant Balliol promised to be Edward's 'man', which meant that Balliol promised to be loyal and to support Edward in all he was asked to do.

Those who try to repair Balliol's reputation argue that previous Scottish kings had sworn fealty to the English king. However, that is to forget the way that Alexander III had asserted his authority over the land of Scotland and how he had drawn a line under the extent of Edward's power in Scotland. The argument that Balliol's promise of loyalty to Edward meant nothing also ignores Edward's clear tactical moves during the Great Cause to gain overlordship and the fact that a feudal oath of loyalty was binding.

Why did Balliol face difficulties in Scotland?

When Balliol became king he took over a country that had been without royal authority for seven years and where the rule of law and royal administration had become weak. Not only that, many Scots nobles disagreed with Edward's choice of king and would do all they could to ignore or undermine Balliol's authority in their regions.

Away from the traditional powerbase of the Lothians and southern Scotland, the power of Scottish kings in the Western Isles and Highlands had always been relatively weak. Now the lords of those far away regions of Scotland felt they could do as they wanted. Balliol lacked power, time and assertiveness to rebuild royal authority in Scotland.

Balliol was in a difficult position. With so many powerful nobles against him, how could he trust them to administer Scotland on his behalf? The answer lay in using members of his own Balliol/Comyn family to fill important posts but that, of course, made relationships with other noble families more difficult.

Nevertheless, Balliol did set up several royal parliaments and appointed his own royal officials to enforce royal authority, not only in friendly areas such as Lothian and Moray but also in more troublesome areas such as Galloway and the Western Isles. Balliol also managed to lessen tension between the Bruce and Comyn families, although the Bruces may just have been waiting for their opportunities.

Balliol needed time to establish himself as king and to let Scotland see how his reign could bring stability, peace and prosperity back again – but it was time that Edward was not prepared to allow Balliol to have.

In what ways did Edward continue to undermine King John?

When the Guardians negotiated the terms of the Treaty of Birgham, they insisted on certain conditions to maintain Scottish independence. One of these was that no English court of law could overturn legal decisions made in Scotland. Of course, the treaty was abandoned with the death of Margaret, and Edward lost no time in taking every opportunity to weaken King John's status.

In 1292 Edward held a parliament in Newcastle. There, a merchant from Berwick made a complaint about a decision taken by the Guardians against him. King John upheld the decision of the Guardians.

That should have been the end of the complaint as the merchant in Berwick was Scottish. Berwick was Scottish and Edward had no legal authority there. However, Edward did intervene, supported the merchant and ordered King John to change his decision. It was clear that Edward had no respect for King John or Scottish independence. The issue of Edward's overlordship and feudal superiority was once again at the heart of English/Scottish relations.

Although King John protested about Edward's actions he soon backed down. King John not only accepted Edward's decision but also announced that the Treaty of Birgham was officially ended and Edward was freed from all and any promises he had made, including the conditions that protected Scottish freedoms and independence.

Edward looking out over 'his' Scotland

Edward took full advantage of the changed relationship between himself and King John. A case similar to that of the merchant of Berwick involved an important noble called Macduff who complained that he had been disinherited from lands he thought should belong to him. The argument seemed to have been settled once Balliol became king but Macduff renewed his complaint. Once again, Edward supported a complaint made against a Scottish decision. King John Balliol was ordered by Edward to appear in person before the English parliament to explain his decision. Clearly Edward was making a point of showing that his authority was greater than Balliol's, despite Scotland being an entirely separate country and beyond Edward's jurisdiction. Despite protests from the Scots, Edward agreed to hear more appeals on cases that had already been decided upon and settled by the Scottish courts. In effect, Edward was stating that he refused to recognise Scotland's right to make and enforce its own laws. Edward was once again asserting his right to be overlord of Scotland, and to treat Scotland as a land over which he had final authority.

And so it went on, with more and more cases being taken to Edward by individuals who were unhappy with the decision of the Scottish courts. Edward continued to undermine Scottish independence by forcing Balliol to accept Edward's men in important positions in the government of Scotland. Edward even redesigned the Royal Seal of Scotland.

War and final conquest?

Why did war break out between Scotland and England?

The immediate cause of war was Scotland's alliance with France, but the roots of the war lay in Edward's treatment of Scotland. Later historians argue that the Guardians could take no more of Edward's bullying tactics, while others argue that Balliol was finally driven into a position where he had to stand up for himself and Scotland. The immediate cause of war came in 1294 when Edward demanded that Scotland pay taxes to finance his war in France **and** supply troops to help him fight it.

The Scots refused to help Edward or to pay for his war. Scotland had no quarrel with France and, in fact, France was an important trading partner with Scotland. Merchants from Flanders in northern France had a large and very important trading base in Berwick.

In 1296 Scotland agreed a treaty with France. Clearly, Edward could not fight a war in France while he faced a threat of invasion from Scotland. Edward now had no option but to deal with the enemy threatening his northern frontier.

Why did the war go so badly for Scotland?

Edward assembled a large army and moved against Berwick. The speed of his advance with such a large army suggests he had been planning his move for a long time. Perhaps war was the final part of his plan to establish complete overlordship over Scotland.

The Scots also reacted quickly and advanced south to reinforce Berwick. Perhaps as many as 10 000 men were gathered to meet the English invasion. The Scots were confident but their confidence was short-lived. The Scottish troops were untested, mostly untrained and poorly equipped. The common army of Scotland was mainly made up of levies – men taken from the farms and small townships of Scotland and ordered to fight as part-payment for the right to farm their land. They were often equipped with little more than sharpened farm tools.

Nevertheless, the Scots took the war to England, raided into north-west England and headed towards Carlisle. English reports from the time described the Scots as people who killed and burned without mercy.

By March 1296 Edward was ready to attack Berwick. Berwick was a well-defended town and resisted Edward's first attacks. To make matters worse the local people insulted and taunted Edward. Edward was furious, and ordered huge war machines to batter down Berwick's defences, then ordered that none of Berwick's defenders should be shown any mercy.

Berwick was soon captured. Reports suggest that soldiers defending Berwick were allowed to leave on condition they did not fight against Edward again. That was part of the rules of war at the time called the Chivalric Code, but there were no such rules protecting the civilian inhabitants of Berwick. English forces began a slaughter of the inhabitants that reports say lasted for three days. In fact one report says the killing only ended when Edward saw a pregnant woman being butchered while giving birth. Edward then ordered the dead and wounded of Berwick to be hung on hooks and spikes around the remaining town walls.

Why did the Scots lose the battle of Dunbar?

After taking Berwick, Edward's forces advanced up the east coast to the next major Scottish strong point – Dunbar Castle. The castle was held by the wife of the Earl of Dunbar, a member of the Comyn family, and therefore a relative of John Balliol.

Meanwhile, a Scottish army had advanced towards Dunbar and had stopped on nearby Doon Hill. From their position the Scots could watch the English prepare for an uphill attack. The Scots held the advantage – then they threw it away!

For some reason the Scots seemed to think the English were retreating rather than preparing for attack. The Scots rushed downhill, lost their advantage and were destroyed by the disciplined English troops.

Why did the Scots fail to resist Edward?

After the defeat at Dunbar the war was all but over. So many Scottish nobles were captured at Dunbar that there was no organised resistance to Edward as he moved north. Edward's tactics at Berwick also helped win the war. As news of the Berwick massacre spread, people living in other towns were terrified as Edward's advance continued. They were ready to surrender as soon as Edward's forces appeared.

Roxburgh Castle surrendered, Jedburgh and Edinburgh were battered to surrender by Edward's siege engines and Stirling Castle was simply abandoned as Edward moved closer. By July Edward was in Elgin, having marched up the entire east coast of Scotland meeting almost no resistance.

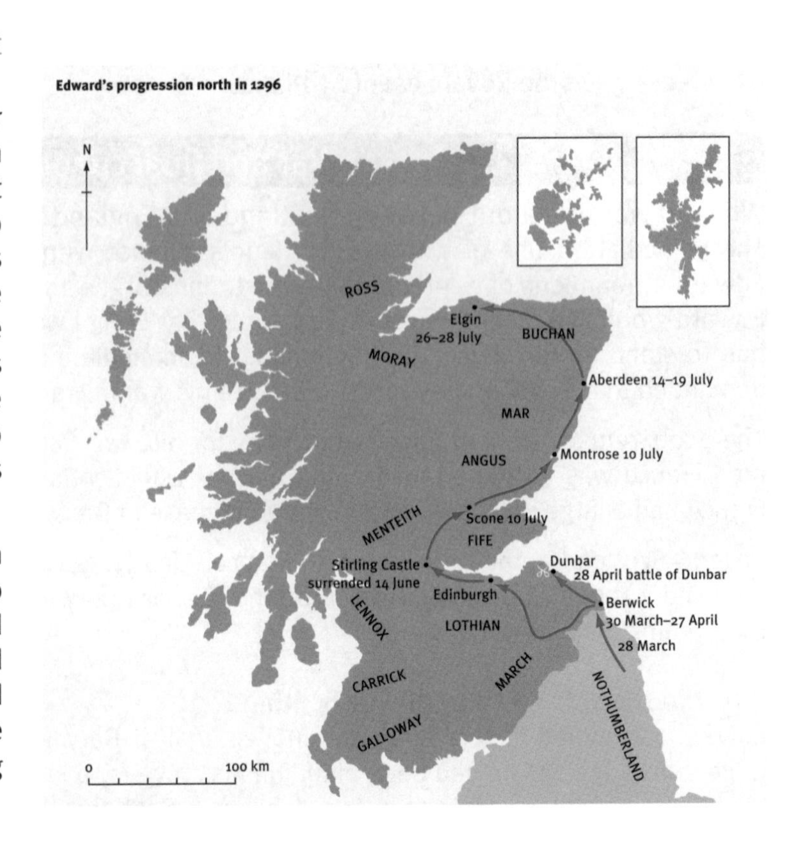

On 2 July 1296 King John Balliol surrendered to Edward. Balliol's apology to Edward was pathetic. He blamed his resistance to Edward on bad advice and his own foolishness. Balliol then claimed that the Scots had surrendered of their own free will and were under no pressure to do so. Balliol ended his apology to Edward by accepting him as overlord of Scotland.

What happened to King John Balliol?

Edward had destroyed the Scottish army and now occupied most of eastern Scotland. Balliol had been defeated and captured. Edward now increased the humiliation. Balliol had the royal coat of arms ripped from his clothing and was then sent to England as a prisoner. Edward eventually released him into the control of the Pope and Balliol lived out the rest of his life on his lands in France. He never returned to Scotland. He became known as Toom Tabard – or Empty Coat – a reference to his loss of title and the removal of the coat of arms.

How did Edward try to destroy Scotland's identity as a separate nation?

Edward was not content with just defeating Balliol's authority. His next actions were aimed at taking away Scotland's identity as a separate and independent nation.

The Stone of Destiny, on which Scottish kings had been crowned, was taken away to London.

The Stone of Destiny

All Scottish legal records went south (and were lost at sea) while all taxes raised in Scotland were taken to London to be spent as Edward wished. The Scottish crown jewels soon followed southwards and Scotland was now referred to as a 'land', not a nation and not a kingdom. As far as Edward was concerned his 'Scottish problem' was over.

In August 1296 Edward put the final seal on his victory. To ensure there was no more trouble Edward insisted that all Scottish nobles must swear an oath of loyalty to him personally. The document that they all signed became known as the Ragman Rolls because of the ragged appearance of the document once all the seals and ribbons of the signatories were attached. Almost all of Scotland's important families now swore an oath of loyalty to Edward, accepting him as their overlord.

Was John Balliol really Toom Tabard – an empty and worthless king?

Several things damned Balliol's chances and historical reputation. The first was his lack of time to establish his authority in Scotland. The second was the growing ambition of the politically and militarily powerful Edward of England. Could any king have stood against Edward at that stage?

Perhaps most importantly, the winners write history and in this case the eventual winner was Robert the Bruce, although that was still some years in the future. We have very little first-hand evidence from this time. What records do exist were often written years after the events they describe. You will read later how Bruce seized the Scottish throne by force. In later years Bruce legitimised his reign by clever and careful propaganda. Part of that legitimising was to make Balliol look as useless and weak as we have come to see him. In other words, after seven centuries most Scots now believe the Bruce version of history!

Issue 3 – William Wallace and Scottish resistance

This issue is about how William Wallace led resistance against Edward's attempts to control Scotland.

To cover the syllabus you should know about the following:

- Why resistance to Edward's rule in Scotland increased.
- The part played by William Wallace and Andrew Murray in the Scottish resistance against Edward.
- The importance of the Scottish victory at Stirling Bridge.
- Whether defeat at Falkirk marked the end of Scottish resistance to Edward.

The growth of Scottish resistance

Why did resistance to Edward's rule grow in Scotland despite Balliol's capture and the defeat of the Scots?

If Edward thought the capture of Balliol would end Scottish resistance, then he was wrong. Edward's attempts to administer Scotland as a part of England led to growing resentment and resistance. In the north, Andrew Murray became a leader of resistance against Edward's rule while in the south of Scotland William Wallace became a focus for resistance.

When Edward appointed his man, John de Warenne, as 'warden of the kingdom and land of Scotland' in August 1296 and gave him responsibility for law and order in the land, Edward further angered many Scots. Edward's mistake was to treat Scotland as a province of England. By using English administrators who had little idea of Scottish laws and customs Edward simply gave a focus to Scottish resentment of English rule. Many of the administrators resented being in Scotland and made no secret of their dislike of the place or the people. Even John de Warenne returned to England after a few months claiming that the Scottish climate was bad for his health.

Another of Edward's officials in Scotland was Hugh de Cressingham – the king's Lord High Treasurer and the man responsible for extracting English taxes in Scotland. Cressingham became known as the most hated man in Scotland. He was pompous and greedy, and even his own side called him a 'son of death'. Cressingham was also at heart an accountant, always looking for the cheapest option in any military action, and that was to lead to disaster for the English.

Edward's officials in Scotland made no attempt to adapt to local customs. They in turn were seen by the local people as part of an army of occupation, to be resisted whenever possible. Even the collection of taxes proved impossible in many areas without the use of force, and that only made hatred of the English occupation all the greater.

Another serious mistake made by Edward was to use certain powerful clans to rule over others. All that policy did was to ignite old clan rivalries. Clan warfare broke out in the Western Isles in April 1297 between the pro-Edward MacDonald family and their jealous neighbours the MacDougals.

In the south-west of Scotland a rising led by Bishop Wishart of Glasgow and Robert Bruce caused problems for Edward, while in the north Andrew Murray's rising was by far the most serious to date.

Given such resentment of English occupation and the lack of strong central government in Scotland for over ten years, it is not surprising to find that resistance and rebellion against the English broke out all over Scotland.

By 1297 there were not one but several rebellions in full swing. Robert Wishart, Bishop of Glasgow, James Stewart, Sir William Douglas, Robert Bruce, William Wallace and Andrew Murray all led uprisings. The bishop and his friends were able to accomplish little, but Wallace and Murray were more successful.

Who was Andrew Murray?

Murray was the son of an important nobleman who owned lands around Avoch, north-west of Inverness. He was a trained soldier and had fought in the Scottish army under Balliol. Murray was captured at the battle of Dunbar but he had escaped and travelled back north, where he found his family lands under English control.

Murray had no trouble assembling a small army and, after an unsuccessful start, he then captured Urquhart, Inverness, Elgin, Duffas and Aberdeen castles. By the end of August 1297 Murray had thrown the English out of northern Scotland, even as far south as Dundee, where he met up with Wallace. They hastily joined forces and marched to Perth. They knew a powerful English army was heading north to crush them but that army had to use Stirling Bridge to get access into northern Scotland. Murray and Wallace made their plans.

Why is Wallace remembered more than Murray?

Most of what we know about Wallace comes from an old poem called 'The Wallace', written by a Scottish poet called Blind Harry about 200 years after Wallace's death. Since the Wallace story we know is based almost entirely on Blind Harry's combination of fact and fiction, **and** since the poem almost ignores Andrew Murray's contribution to the Scottish resistance, it is hardly surprising that Murray's rising in the north of Scotland has been almost forgotten.

What do we know about Wallace's early life?

Almost nothing is known about Wallace until his name appears on an English list of outlaws. He was accused of murdering William de Hazelrig, the English sheriff at Lanark.

There is still doubt about whether or not his family was important enough to have signed the Ragman Rolls or whether his family refused to sign as an indication of continued resistance to the English. Either way, it really does not matter. What is significant is that William Wallace led sustained resistance to the English and was, along with Murray, victorious over a much larger English army at the battle of Stirling Bridge.

The battle of Stirling Bridge

Why were so many battles fought in the area around Stirling at this time?

Even today the main transport routes between south and north Scotland hinge around the Stirling area.

In medieval times the easiest route from England to Scotland was up the east coast. Armies marched from Berwick northwards, skirting the Lammermuir Hills, past Dunbar and then across the relatively flat Lothians to Edinburgh. Then there was a problem – how to get further north? The Firth of Forth was an impassable obstacle to armies and all had to march upstream until they reached the first bridge across the Forth. That bridge was at Stirling, near to Stirling Castle.

Control of that bridge was vital, both to attackers and defenders. By 11 September 1297 the English army was camped on the southern side of the Forth, near the castle. Hidden just across the river in the woods covering Abbey Craig was the Scottish army, led by Wallace and Murray. From their position high up in the wooded hillside the Scots had a clear view of the English camp and their preparations to cross the river.

How did the two sides prepare for battle at Stirling Bridge?

The English army that arrived at Stirling numbered about 7000 men, including about 1000 on horseback. The force was led by the Earl of Surrey and Hugh de Cressingham. While the latter was an experienced manager of Edward's administration of Scotland, he had very little military experience. Surrey was indeed a military commander, but he was in bad health just before the battle.

Crossing the bridge at Stirling was a difficult military manoeuvre. Only three mounted knights could cross the bridge at one time so the army would be in a slow-moving bottleneck while they crossed. Cressingham had been told about a nearby ford where sixty knights could cross in a line at one time but he rejected that option. Cressingham wanted the battle over quickly so he could disband the army soon afterwards and save money by not paying more wages than he had to.

Cressingham feared that the Scottish army would vanish back into the hills if the English army crossed the Forth by using the ford a short distance away. The campaign would then drag on – costing the English treasury more money. To be fair, Cressingham also knew that to make his army wade through a river as powerful as the Forth while under enemy attack could be a recipe for disaster.

Facing the English army were the followers of Wallace and Murray. In total the Scots numbered about 2500 and most were armed with long poles called pikes. The pikes were about 5 metres long with sharp blades attached to the top. These pikemen were trained to fight in tight formations called schiltrons. With hundreds of men huddled together in the formation, each one holding out their pikes, schiltrons were like giant hedgehogs, bristling with lethal blades and almost impossible to break with cavalry charges.

A schiltron

Schiltrons did however have one big disadvantage. If they remained in one place they provided an easy target for archers, who could rain down arrows on top of the mass of men. However, Wallace had thought of that problem. The Scottish schiltrons that waited on Abbey Craig had been trained to move as a unit and the mobility of the schiltrons was to surprise the English forces.

How did the battle start?

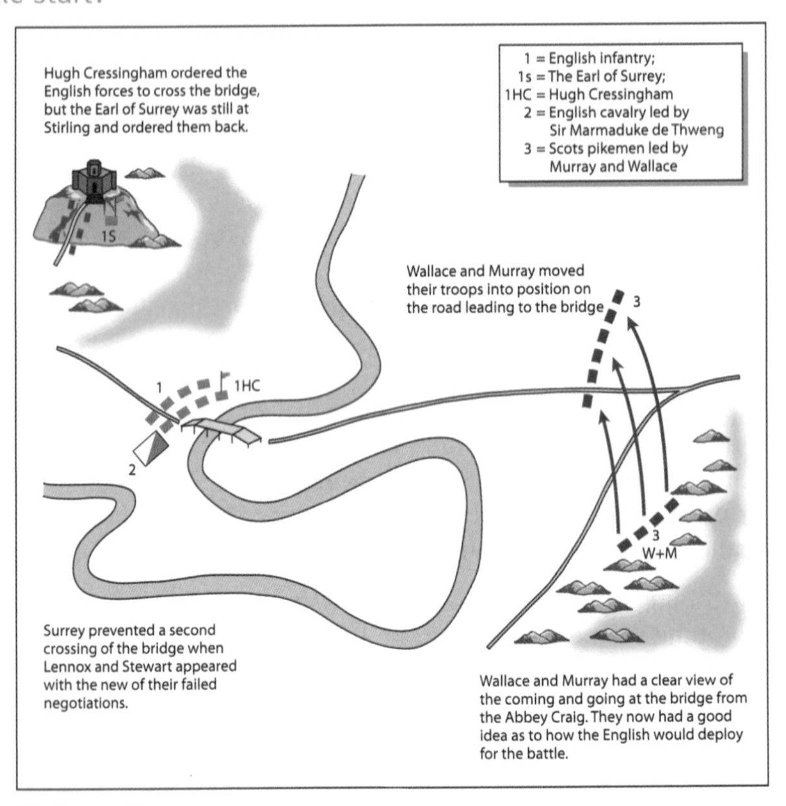

Starting positions

When the English army began to cross the bridge their plans soon became chaotic. After two false starts, with the army starting to cross the bridge, taking up their battle positions and then being called back, Wallace and Murray were in no doubt about how the English army would line up for battle.

Some English commanders warned Cressingham that the Scots now knew exactly what the English battle formations were and suggested that some knights should cross the river by the ford and outflank the Scots. Once again Cressingham ignored good tactical advice.

What happened at the battle of Stirling Bridge?

The battle began with the Scottish schiltrons advancing downhill out of the woods. Less than half of the English force had crossed the river and few were ready for battle. By attacking quickly the Scots had trapped the English forces and cut them off from the bridge, their only means of retreat.

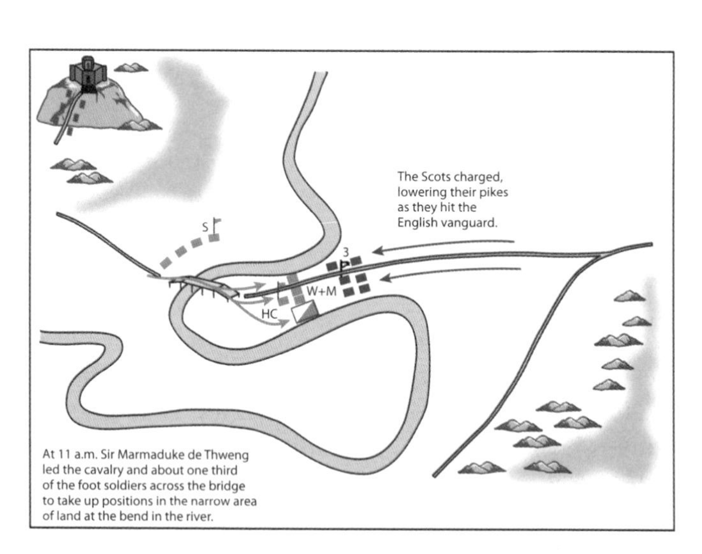

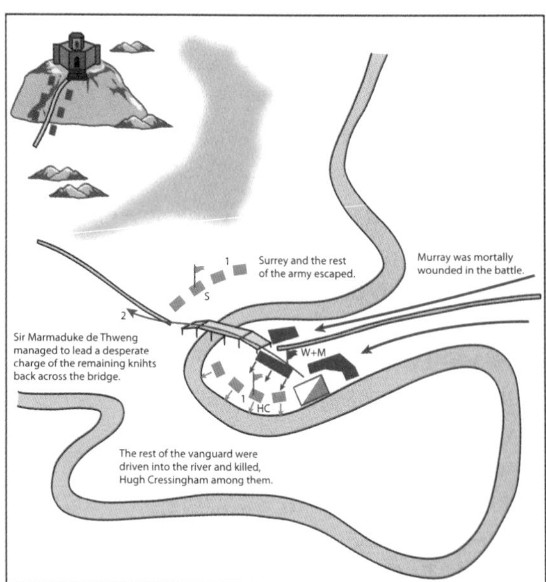

The English cavalry, led by Sir Marmaduke de Thweng, made a desperate charge towards the bridge and managed to reach safety but the English foot soldiers were trapped. Thousands of English soldiers died on the points of the pikes or drowned while trying to swim to safety. According to stories after the battle, when Hugh de Cressingham was captured he was flayed alive. That means his skin stripped from his flesh and was then used to make souvenirs for the victorious Scots.

Although the English who had not yet crossed the bridge still outnumbered the Scots, their confidence had gone. The English army retreated all the way back to Berwick, taking their commander, the Earl of Surrey, with them. An English force under Sir Marmaduke de Thweng tried to hold Stirling Castle against the Scots but they surrendered after a few weeks.

How far was victory for the Scots at Stirling Bridge the result of English failures?

Wallace and Murray chose their battleground well, but they were helped hugely by English overconfidence, poor planning and Cressingham's desire to save money.

By choosing such a poor battle site the English lost all their advantage of size and military strength. Cressingham foolishly rejected sensible advice from more able commanders. He placed his advancing forces into a bottleneck from which they could not escape. Cressingham's desire to save money, combined with Surrey's expectation of an easy victory just like at Dunbar, were the real reasons for English defeat and Scots victory. The English commanders simply were overconfident and underestimated the Scots. Perhaps, they could be forgiven for that – after all, the English leaders could remember the chaotic Scottish army that they had defeated at Dunbar two years earlier.

How important was the battle of Stirling Bridge to the Wars of Independence?

In the longer term the battle of Stirling Bridge was of very little importance to the Wars of Independence. In the short term it gave a huge morale boost to the Scots, but it did not drive the English from Scotland. Although Stirling Bridge was a defeat for the English, it also taught them a lesson. Wallace had declared his presence as a major threat to English control in Scotland. When Edward came back north for revenge the English would not underestimate the Scots again.

The aftermath of Stirling Bridge

Why was Wallace made Guardian of Scotland?

Strictly speaking Wallace was made joint leader of the army of Scotland and Guardian along with Andrew Murray, but Murray had been seriously wounded in the battle and died soon afterwards.

Some writers have expressed surprise that the nobles of Scotland allowed Wallace, a low-born former outlaw to become a Guardian, but was it such a surprise? Wallace had proven himself to be a winner. By not signing the Ragman Roll (whether by accident or design) Wallace could be seen as having been consistently strong in his opposition to the invading English.

Nor was Wallace a threat to the Scottish nobility. At no point did Wallace seek power for himself. He always worked to restore Scotland's strength on behalf of its absent king, John Balliol. Naturally the Comyn/Balliol families were happy with this position. They also knew that as long as Wallace was Guardian then the ambitions of the Bruce family would be held in check.

As long as Wallace went on fighting he took all the risks and the nobility of Scotland could sit back and reap the benefits. There was therefore little opposition to the move to make Wallace 'Sir William' and joint Guardian of Scotland

How well did Wallace govern Scotland?

Wallace had relatively little time to build up Scotland's strength before the English fought back. Little documentary evidence remains and, as a result, historians have spent much time analysing a letter sent by Wallace and Murray to the port of Lübeck in present-day Germany. The letter makes clear that Scotland was once again 'open for business' as an independent nation. It asserts that the English had been driven out of Scotland and, in effect, the letter is a piece of necessary propaganda. Scotland needed to build up its strength and the only way to do that was to restore trading links. When Edward destroyed Berwick he also destroyed the confidence that foreign traders had about investing in Scotland. Wallace knew that trade was vital, especially across the northern North Sea which the English did not control.

The letter is also important in that it states clearly that Wallace and Murray were commanders of the Scottish army only, and that they recognised the kingship of King John.

The battle of Falkirk

Why did the battle of Falkirk go so badly wrong for the Scots?

By the summer of 1298 Edward was back in Scotland looking for revenge. However, he had little clear idea where Wallace was. Edward's army was tired, hungry and disheartened. Edward was about to return to Edinburgh to resupply when he heard that Wallace was near Falkirk, hoping to launch hit-and-run raids against the retreating English force. Edward changed his plans and advanced towards Wallace at Falkirk.

There is still doubt about why Wallace chose to fight where he did. Some say Wallace was goaded into fighting by his nobles, who claimed it would be cowardly to run away. Others argue that Wallace was surprised by the sudden arrival of Edward, who moved quickly towards Falkirk.

Neither argument holds much water. Wallace would have been unlikely to fight a risky pitched battle on a matter of personal pride. The second argument is also weak. An army cannot just change direction immediately and if Wallace really was watching the retreating English prior to raiding its baggage trains his scouts would have told him of the change in English plans.

Perhaps another argument is more convincing, and that is that the real military brain that had brought victory at Stirling Bridge belonged to Murray. Without Murray, Wallace made serious tactical mistakes that led to defeat.

How did the two sides compare at the battle of Falkirk?

The English army that advanced towards Falkirk was much stronger than the one that fell apart at Stirling Bridge. There were more than 2000 cavalry, large numbers of archers and around 15 000 foot soldiers. Many of them were battle-hardened troops from Edward's war in France. At the head of the army rode Edward I, a master tactician and a man determined to have his revenge.

Facing Edward stood a Scottish army of around 500 cavalry and about 6000 pikemen, grouped into three large schiltrons. Between the schiltrons stood Scottish archers. The Scots held high ground and, although they were outnumbered, a good battle plan could have made a big difference. As it turned out, Wallace's battle plan was weak.

What happened at the battle of Falkirk?

In front of the schiltrons there was a large marshy bog and behind the Scots there was a wooded hillside. Some military historians suggest that the position was meant to deter the English knights from attacking at full gallop. However, the English were no fools and simply moved around the bog, attacking the Scots at their left and right wings. The Scottish cavalry seems to have fought bravely and to have done what they could against the massive English onslaught but they soon retreated. In fact, their retreat was so fast some reports suggested the Scottish horsemen simply ran away. Whatever the truth is, the Scottish cavalry played no further part in the battle.

Whether or not the Scots expected a cavalry attack on their flanks is unclear, but while the huge schiltrons easily saw off the English cavalry, the pikemen also hid the charging cavalry from the Scottish archers until it was too late. The archers were caught in open ground and were slaughtered.

Edward saw his chance. The Scottish schiltrons had little room to move and simply stood their ground. They were sitting targets for the English archers, who poured storms of arrows into the massed Scots schiltrons.

To this day it is not known why Wallace made the tactical mistake of leaving his schiltrons stranded in the open to face the English arrows. At Stirling Bridge and later at Bannockburn the schiltrons consisted of mobile, trained men who moved as a huge bristling mass. Clearly it was possible to train for, and plan, such mobility so why it was not done at Falkirk is a mystery.

Once the schiltrons collapsed under the hail of arrows, it was easy for the cavalry to cut down the running Scots. Wallace was hurried away from the battlefield but his credibility as a successful war leader was over.

Wallace and the Scottish resistance after Falkirk

What happened to Wallace after Falkirk?

After the battle of Falkirk, Wallace resigned the Guardianship.

In defeat, Wallace had little support. He was no longer seen as a lucky war leader. The Scottish nobility had tolerated Wallace as Guardian of Scotland just as long as he won victories. Two new Guardians were appointed to work together and, in a sense, Scotland was back to where it had been before Wallace's rising. Edward was victorious and Scotland was again under the influence of the Bruce and Comyn families when the two family heads, Robert Bruce and John Comyn, became joint Guardians of Scotland.

In the years after the defeat at Falkirk Wallace seems to have travelled to Europe to plead the case for Scotland in France and with the Pope, but little is known for certain.

Why was there less resistance in Scotland to Edward I by 1304?

Wallace returned to Scotland in 1303 but by the summer of 1304 he had outlived his usefulness. Edward had learned from his earlier mistakes. He realised he had made an error of judgement when he tried to crush Scotland after Balliol was captured. By trying to destroy Scotland's identity as a nation and put his own English managers in charge of 'the land' of Scotland, Edward had simply provoked outrage and resistance. Now Edward decided to get the Scottish nobles on his side. All Scottish nobles with the exception of Wallace were offered an amnesty as long as they promised loyalty to Edward. In the 'Ordinance for the order of Scotland' issued in September 1305 Edward declared that Scots noblemen could keep their lands and again become sheriffs, this time enforcing English laws. In exchange for this the Scots lords had to stop their rebellion, accept Edward as king and swear allegiance.

Even John Comyn, one of the main leaders of the resistance to Edward, accepted Edward's offer of peace. It was as if the Scottish resistance had never happened.

In return for his generosity Edward gained benefits. The Comyn family and all its branches now became loyal supporters of Edward and all demands for a return of King John Balliol were forgotten.

Why was Wallace executed so horribly?

Edward had made it known that the only person he would not forgive was Wallace, and that any person helping Wallace would also face the anger of Edward. Almost inevitably Wallace was betrayed. On 3 August 1304 Wallace was captured, his hiding place betrayed by Sir John Menteith. Wallace was taken to London and put on trial for treason. Wallace protested that he had never accepted Edward as his king and never sworn loyalty to him.

Wallace stood trial with no right of defence and the verdict was never in doubt. Edward had decided Wallace had to be made an example of so as to discourage any future rebellion.

Wallace was sentenced to be hanged, drawn, quartered, then disembowelled and beheaded. His head was sent to the Tower of London while the rest of his body was quartered. Newcastle, Berwick, Stirling and Perth were each sent a quarter of his body as a warning to those who might think of rebelling against Edward I.

How important was Wallace to Scottish independence?

From one point of view Wallace was not important. After one victory that inspired Scottish resistance, his next battle was an outright defeat that demoralised the Scots and led to English domination once again.

English chroniclers described Wallace as a murdering bandit who deserved his fate. Such comments could be expected coming as they did from English sources, but Scottish chroniclers make little mention of Wallace either. Menteith, the man who betrayed Wallace, suffered no punishment from the Scots. A few years later Bruce rewarded him with lands and titles.

Finally, Wallace had never had much support from Scottish nobility. His continued resistance to Edward after Falkirk kept Edward angry and the Scots' position remained difficult. In short, Wallace had become an annoying embarrassment. There was not even public protest at Wallace's death or the display of his body parts.

So why then does Wallace live on in folk memory as a Scottish hero? Blind Harry's poem was written almost 200 years after Wallace's death, so how did Blind Harry even know about Wallace and why did he write an epic poem about him? It is supposed that Wallace must have meant much to Scots for his memory to live on, but there is no strong evidence to support that claim. With little evidence about Wallace it is very difficult to draw strong conclusions, but very easy to build up stories and legends around him!

One final point is to think about where our primary evidence comes from. Most of the accounts of this time were written years later, when Bruce and his successors were in power. It seems only likely that tales of the Wars of Independence would boost the role of Robert the Bruce rather than someone fighting to restore John Balliol. Consequently, tales of Wallace may have been 'airbrushed' from history. However, why is it that when Blind Harry came to write his epic poem about Wallace, there were still stories and legends and interest about Wallace 200 years after his death? Clearly, Wallace cannot be dismissed as an irrelevance to the Wars of Independence in either life or death.

Issue 4 – The rise and triumph of Robert the Bruce

This issue is about how Robert the Bruce became king of Scotland and then went on to regain Scottish independence.

To cover the syllabus you should know about the following:

- How Bruce became king of Scotland.
- How Bruce led the Scots to victory at Bannockburn.
- How Bruce established himself as 'Good King Robert' within Scotland.
- How Bruce gained international recognition for Scotland as a free and independent nation before his death in 1328.

The rise of Robert the Bruce

How true is the image of Bruce as a national hero?

By the 1320s Robert the Bruce was, to many Scots, a victorious war leader and was even called 'Good King Robert'. To most Scots today, Robert the Bruce is a national hero who won the Wars of Independence, defeated Edward and 'sent him homeward to think again'. A version of his face has been on Scottish banknotes and on national stamps.

On the other hand, it is also true that Bruce was only the latest (and most successful) member of his family to plot and plan for power, as previous generations of Bruces had done before him. Bruce was certainly involved in a murder that led to his seizing the throne of Scotland for himself. His actions also led to years of imprisonment and sudden death for members of his family.

At the time of the Great Cause, Robert the Bruce's grandfather had been one of the claimants for the throne after the death of Margaret. In the years that followed, Bruce had been made Guardian after the resignation of Wallace but had changed sides to support Edward on separate occasions when he felt it suited his best interests. In short, the Bruce family, like the Comyn family, was ambitious and wanted the throne for their own family.

Why were John Comyn and Robert the Bruce rivals?

Quite simply, they were the heads of Scotland's two most ambitious families. Both wanted the throne of Scotland. The Comyns were closely related to Balliol, and Bruce's grandfather had been one of the competitors claiming the throne when Margaret, Maid of Norway, died.

Bruce disliked Comyn. Two years before Comyn surrendered to Edward, Bruce had already changed sides yet again and become a supporter of Edward in exchange for keeping his lands and titles for the Bruce family. As one of the first Scottish nobles to make peace, even before the Ordinance of Scotland, Bruce expected big rewards from Edward. He was soon furious because Comyn and his family gained all the top jobs and there were rumours Bruce was about to lose his lands in the south-west of Scotland. By 1304–05 Bruce was resentful and jealous of John Comyn.

Critics have argued Robert the Bruce was unreliable and treacherous, breaking promises and changing sides when it suited him. There is some truth in this. Bruce signed the Ragman Rolls promising loyalty to Edward, only to then lead resistance to the English king, before surrendering again in 1297. After Wallace's defeat at Falkirk, Bruce became joint Guardian of Scotland with John Comyn but he resigned the Guardianship and he was one of the first to make peace with Edward. Then, after Wallace's execution, Bruce became a focus of resistance to the English. However, Bruce was also consistent, in that his ambitions lay within his family. Some even argue Bruce was driven by personal ambition alone, given what he allowed to happen to his family later on.

Did Bruce plan to seize the throne of Scotland?

There is no evidence to prove that Bruce had a precise plan to grab the crown for himself, but there is evidence that Bruce was plotting and planning to increase his influence.

Bruce was well aware that he needed as wide a base of support as he could get. He knew the importance of the Scottish Church leaders. He also knew that those Church leaders were concerned about the increasing power of Edward, and consequently the spreading influence of the English Church.

In a secret meeting at Cambuskenneth Abbey near Falkirk on 11 June 1304 an agreement was reached between Bruce and the Scottish bishops, including Lamberton and Wishart. Each side promised to support the other. It is unclear exactly what was meant by 'support', but if either side broke their promise a penalty of £10 000 had to be paid.

Bruce was well aware of this arrangement when he met with Comyn at the Church of Grey Friars. There is no way of telling what happened at the meeting with Comyn but it is certainly unlikely that Bruce planned a murder in a church on the strength of the meeting with Lamberton and Wishart.

Why did Bruce murder John Comyn?

Robert the Bruce and John Comyn represented the two families who most wanted the throne for themselves. Comyn was of course related to John Balliol.

In February 1306, Bruce and Comyn met at the Church of the Grey Friars in Dumfries. No one is sure what happened there but when Bruce left the meeting Comyn lay dying and a Bruce follower went back into the church to 'mac sicaar' (make sure) and finish the job. Historians can only guess what they argued about. Was it their ambitions to be king? Was it to rise up yet again against the English? The purpose of the meeting is not so important. The result of the meeting was vital to the future of Scotland.

Why did the murder of John Comyn almost destroy Bruce and his family?

Bruce had murdered a man in a church. That was a sin of sacrilege and for that crime Bruce would surely be excommunicated. Excommunication meant that, according to the Church, Bruce would burn in hell for eternity when he died. More immediately and perhaps more importantly, if the order of excommunication were served on Bruce by the Church in Scotland then all oaths of loyalty to Bruce would be cancelled. He would lose his power. Bruce had to act quickly. He had friends in high places in the Scottish Church, especially Bishop Wishart. The Scottish Church prized its independence from English control and Wishart saw in Bruce a man who would help maintain the Church's independence, so it was he who delayed and avoided excommunicating Bruce.

Excommunication would also deny Bruce the chance to be crowned king of Scots: here again Wishart helped Bruce by pardoning him. At Scone on 25 March 1306 Bruce was crowned king by the Countess of Buchan. Bruce's actions had offended many Scots nobles, and others were scared of the consequences if they supported Bruce. Was there any point attending a coronation that would infuriate the Church, Edward of England, the Comyns and all their allies? It seemed that Bruce had no chance of long-term success.

After Bruce led some small-scale raids into Fife, an English/Comyn force under Aymer de Valence, John Comyn's brother-in-law, hunted him. In June, Bruce's small army was setting up camp in Methven woods. There the English force ambushed them and Bruce's army was almost wiped out. Bruce himself only just escaped. With only a few surviving followers, Bruce, the crowned king of Scotland, was now on the run.

Across Scotland the relatives and friends of the Comyn family made it their business to hunt down Robert the Bruce. At Dalry in Ayrshire Bruce's followers were defeated again and Bruce was forced to sail away from mainland Scotland and go into hiding.

There are more guesses than facts about where Robert went in the winter of 1306–07. The only thing that seemed guaranteed was that Bruce was finished. He had no land, no army and few supporters. English chroniclers of the time refer to Bruce as King Hob – meaning King Nobody.

Meanwhile, without Robert the Bruce to punish, English vengeance turned on Bruce's family. His female relatives were captured, having escaped north before Kildrummy Castle was taken. Robert's wife, sister and daughter were then held separately in almost solitary confinement in different manor houses and nunneries for almost ten years. The Countess of Buchan, who had crowned Bruce king of Scotland, and one of Robert's sisters, Mary, were left in cages hanging from the walls of Berwick and Roxburgh castles respectively. Even more serious punishment was reserved for the males of the family. Neil, brother of Robert the Bruce, was executed along with other supporters of Bruce. They were hanged, drawn and quartered.

How did Bruce manage to recover his power and authority in Scotland?

The short answer is that Bruce got lucky. His biggest break was the death of Edward I in July 1307.

In the months before Edward's death Bruce had landed on the coast of his old lands in south-west Scotland. There he managed to raise a small army and to win some minor skirmishes at Glen Trool in April and at Loudoun Hill in May, but not before two more of his brothers were captured and executed. Other smaller victories were won but all that happened was that Edward I grew angrier. By this time Edward was old and ill. He wanted one last advance into Scotland to crush Bruce, but while leading his army he died at Burgh on Sands on the Solway Firth.

Edward's son (now Edward II) led the army back into England. Bruce now had some breathing space and time to deal with his enemies in Scotland.

How did Bruce defeat his enemies in Scotland?

Bruce had to remove the threat from the Comyn family if he were to remain king. Bruce also knew that as long as Scotland remained divided between his supporters and those of Comyn it would be impossible to organise united resistance against the English.

The centre of Comyn power lay in the north-east of Scotland, and in the winter of 1307–08 Bruce was there, attacking both English and Comyn bases. After taking several Comyn castles in the Great Glen and then Inverness, the Earl of Ross, a Comyn ally, made a truce with Bruce.

The war in the north-east continued into the winter. Bruce was exhausted and fell ill. In a boggy forest at Slioch the Earl of Buchan cornered Bruce's army. Bruce seemed to be finished but once again luck played a part. It was Christmas Day 1307 and the Earl of Buchan refused to push on with his attack. A week later, when Buchan returned, Bruce had recovered enough to lead his men out to face Buchan. Discouraged by Bruce's recovery, Buchan retreated.

By the spring of 1308 Bruce was even stronger. The Comyn and English forces seemed unable to coordinate a campaign against Bruce and in March the armies of Bruce and Buchan came face to face again, this time at Inverurie. The battle of Inverurie was a decisive victory for Bruce. After winning the battle Bruce ordered all the lands of the Earl of Buchan to be destroyed. The 'Herschip of Buchan', as the destruction of Comyn lands was called, destroyed the Comyn powerbase. People loyal to Comyn were killed, animals and crops destroyed and property was burned to the ground. Bruce's campaign against the Comyns in the north-east and then 'the Herschip of Buchan' meant that Bruce had almost won his civil war.

While Bruce had been in the north-east, Sir William Douglas and Bruce's last surviving brother were in the south-west and the Western Isles. Here Bruce faced resistance from the powerful MacDougal family. The MacDougals were Lords of the Western Isles and had long seen themselves as independent of the Scottish kings. In fact the Western Isles had only joined the Scottish kingdom in 1266. Bruce asserted his power with speed and violence. In late 1309, at the battle of the Pass of Brander, Bruce destroyed the power of the MacDougals.

How did Bruce increase his power from 1309 onwards?

By 1309 Bruce had defeated his enemies in Scotland and he used his parliament at St Andrews to start a propaganda campaign aimed at justifying himself as king. In the Declaration of the Clergy, Scotland's bishops accepted Bruce as the legitimate Scottish king. Once again they forgave him for the sacrilegious murder of Comyn. At the same time Scottish nobles apparently issued their own declaration giving their full support to Bruce's kingship. That document, however, no longer exists.

Certainly by 1309 Bruce seemed safe within Scotland as its king. Even the French king sent word that he recognised Bruce as Scottish king, rightfully replacing the absent John Balliol. However, although the civil war in Scotland seemed to be settled, the war with England was not.

Edward II did not have his father's military talents but he was still not prepared to let Scotland slip from his grasp. Meanwhile the military skills of Bruce had been developed in the years of struggle after 1306.

Bruce knew that his army was unlikely to win a pitched battle with Edward II so the Scottish king developed his 'secret war' – what we would call guerrilla warfare. He launched sudden surprise attacks then vanished into the hills and forests again. Time and again, when English armies marched into

Scotland, they were forced to retreat as a result of Bruce burning and destroying any food, shelter or water that could help the enemy. Meanwhile Scottish troops raided into northern England. Not only did the Scots return with all the loot and livestock they could bring back, the persistent Scottish attacks into England increased pressure on Edward. English nobles in the north of England asked why their king could not protect them.

By 1314, Edward was facing the possibility of being forced out of Scotland. Most of Scotland's major castles, including Dundee, Perth, Dumfries, Linlithgow, Roxburgh and Edinburgh, had been retaken by the end of 1313. Only Stirling and Berwick castles remained in English hands. At Stirling, the castle was under siege by the Scots. Sir Philip Mowbray held the castle for the English but he agreed to surrender the castle to the Scots if King Edward II had not come to relieve him by Midsummer Day 1314.

Edward II could not let Stirling Castle surrender without making an attempt to break the siege, so in the summer of 1314 he marched north with a huge army. The scene was set for the battle of Bannockburn.

The battle of Bannockburn

How did each side prepare for battle?

By the middle of June 1314, Edward II's army was approaching Stirling Castle. In the army there were about 15 000 foot soldiers, 1000 archers and 2000 cavalry. Facing the advancing English force was a Scottish army of about 5000 men. As medieval battles went, the English should have won easily but instead they lost. Why?

The Scots waiting in the woods near Bannockburn were organised, well-trained and confident. They had not faced defeat under Bruce for a very long time. Bruce's men were grouped in three huge schiltrons of about 1500 men in each. The Scots had a clearly understood chain of command and a plan that made excellent use of the terrain. Using the ground around the Bannockburn to their advantage helped make up for the difference in size between the smaller Scottish army and the larger opposing force.

In contrast, the English lacked coherent organisation. Edward appointed many of his friends to important positions in the army, regardless of the military experience they may or may not have had. He also removed army commanders if he did not like them personally, even if they had long experience and proven talent as military leaders.

The English advanced into an area the Scots had prepared well as a potential battlefield.

Bruce was determined to deny the English use of the old Roman road that led straight to Stirling Castle along a high dry ridge for their advance. Bruce knew that once the advancing English crossed the Bannockburn there were hills to the left and a narrow area of flat, rough ground to the right that stretched off into the 'carse', an area of rough boggy marshland that was bounded by the Bannockburn and the Firth of Forth. Bruce wanted to force the English onto that carse so he ordered potholes (called potts) to be dug on and around the road to make the road almost unusable to the advancing forces.

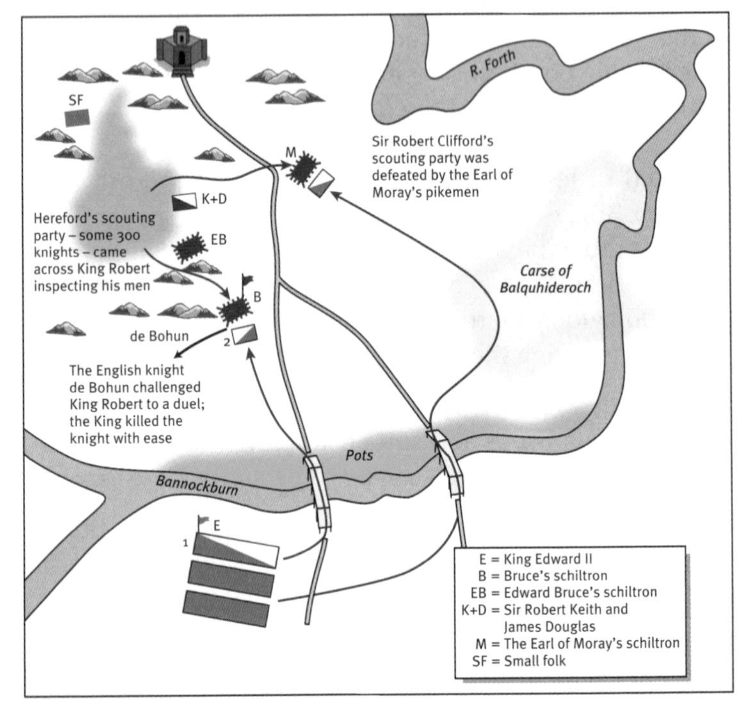

The battle of Bannockburn

Why were the Scots encouraged after the first contact with the English forces?

As the English army advanced towards the Bannockburn, Bruce was still not committed to do battle. The Scots were hidden in the woods of the King's Park and could have slipped away unseen if they wished.

The first contact between the Scots and English forces happened almost by accident. A force of about 300 English cavalry rode up the road, avoiding the potts as best they could. Their intention was to scout the land ahead and if possible make contact with the garrison in Stirling Castle. Suddenly the English cavalry found Bruce out in the open inspecting his troops and unaware that English troops were anywhere nearby. For brief seconds neither side knew what to do. Suddenly a lone English knight called Henry de Bohun saw his chance for fame and glory and charged at Bruce. De Bohun was a fully-armed experienced knight on a warhorse. Bruce was lightly armed on a much smaller horse and not expecting to fight. As the English knight charged closer the whole future of Scotland hung in the balance.

Bruce sat still on his horse until the last minute, when he moved his horse slightly to the side of de Bohun's charge, stood in his stirrups and crashed his battle-axe into the head of de Bohun. The Englishman fell dead to the ground. Enraged, the rest of the English cavalry charged but by this time the Scottish schiltron had moved from the woods to defend their king. The cavalry crashed against the wall of pikes and failed to break through. The English retreated to the sound of Scots cheers.

While the combat between Bruce and de Bohun was taking place, the main English force under Sir Robert Clifford had left the main road and moved eastwards to explore an alternative route across the carse towards the castle. However the path was poor quality, steep sided and really not suitable for heavy use.

To counter the English advance a Scottish schiltron led by Thomas Randolph, the Earl of Moray, moved out of the woods and positioned itself in the path of the advancing English. Arguments broke out between two English commanders in Clifford's force. The experienced Sir Thomas Grey wanted to attack quickly, before the Scots were fully prepared. On the other hand Sir Henry Beaumont wanted to delay an attack until he saw the full Scottish battle position. Of course, the delay gave the Scots time to prepare their schiltron formation fully. Without waiting for further orders the cavalry under Sir Thomas charged at the Scots only to be met with a forest of pikes. The rest of the English force had no choice but to support the now stranded Sir Thomas. The Scots stood firm, their schiltron was unbreakable and the English knights either died on the Scottish pikes or rode around the schiltron ineffectually and with growing frustration.

That night, as the English regrouped on open boggy ground, English morale was at rock bottom. Bruce had killed de Bohun and twice Scottish schiltrons had forced English cavalry to retreat with heavy casualties.

Why did Bruce decide to fight on the second day?

Even after the successes of the first day, the Scots were still not confident of victory. The English army was growing bigger as more troops arrived during the night. Bruce was reluctant to fight a full-scale battle. If he lost the battle then everything he had achieved would vanish.

The Scots were preparing to retreat from Bannockburn and resume hit-and-run tactics when news reached them of the disorganised and miserable state of the English forces. Bruce decided to fight. It was all or nothing.

What happened on the second day of the battle of Bannockburn?

During midsummer in central Scotland it hardly gets dark. In the early hours of the morning the Scottish schiltrons advanced out of the High Wood; then suddenly all the Scots knelt to be blessed by the Bishop of Arbroath. Reports from the English camp suggest that Edward II believed the Scots were begging for mercy. They were not! The plan of the Scots was to keep pushing forward with the heavy schiltrons knowing the English had little room to manoeuvre their forces.

English preparations were chaotic. As the cavalry lined up at the front of the army they saw their options being closed down by the rapidly advancing schiltrons. The power of charging cavalry is the momentum they build up in their charge, but step-by-step the Scots were reducing what little momentum there was to be gained by the English charge.

The English seemed to have learned nothing from the experiences of the day before. Once again the cavalry set off on a ragged charge but the Scottish schiltrons stayed solid and began to push steadily forward. The front ranks of the English force were forced back only to meet the rest of the English force crowding up behind them. The Scots knew the English were trapped and crowded together, with the steep-sided Bannockburn behind them and the advancing Scots in front of them. The English commanders had no room to deploy their archers to wreck the schiltrons as had happened at Falkirk.

Some archers did manage to form up and threaten the schiltron which was led by Bruce but the Scottish cavalry under Sir Robert Keith soon scattered the archers.

The English army was trapped, dazed and confused. In fact the sheer size of the English force had been a disadvantage. The final stage in the battle came when the English saw what appeared to be another Scottish army charging down from nearby Coxet Hill. Later historians call this 'new army' the small people or 'wee folk'. Where this force came from no one is quite sure. Some say it was made up of cooks, women and the families of the fighting men who charged downhill to give the Scots support just when the English looked to be on the point of collapse. Other historians argue they were Highland forces who had arrived late for the battle. Either way, the sight of apparently fresh forces arriving was the final straw for the English and they began a headlong retreat back across the Bannockburn, slipping, sliding and drowning as they fled.

Edward II escaped but thousands of English soldiers did not. Reports from the time refer to huge numbers of English soldiers dying as they tried to cross the Bannockburn and run to safety.

Why did the English lose the battle of Bannockburn?

Historians still argue about whether the Scots won a great victory or if the English caused their own defeat.

English errors included overconfidence, a confused command structure made worse by Edward II dabbling in military planning he did not fully understand and an utter failure to learn from mistakes on the first day of the battle. Why did the English not learn from Falkirk that the way to deal with schiltrons, mobile or not, was to deploy archers, defended by cavalry, and send wave after wave of arrows into them?

Finally, on top of those problems, why did the English army, well equipped with scouts and moving over a landscape they knew well, move their forces onto boggy land on which their room for manoeuvre was severely restricted by the Bannockburn and the Firth of Forth?

Was the Scottish victory the result of careful planning?

Those who claim that Scottish planning won the battle do have some strong arguments. Remember, the whole point of the English advance was to relieve Stirling Castle. They had to get there, and the Scots knew that.

Scottish control over the high road to Stirling was vital for victory. By digging the potts around the high road, the Scots forced the advancing English to look for alternative routes. Faced with hills to their right, covered in forest and full of a waiting enemy, the English had no choice but to head out onto the carse and into boggy ground.

The Scottish troops were well trained. Remember these groups of pikemen were huge – over 1000 men in each – and there were at least three if not four such groups on the battlefield. By keeping the schiltrons pushing forward the Scots gave the English no room to move or to regroup. The English were always on the back foot. As in a rugby scrum, the pack being pushed back found it almost impossible to stop the momentum of the other pack and regain a forward push itself.

Bruce also knew how to use his cavalry to prevent English archers from threatening his schiltrons. The Scots cavalry were used intelligently where and when they were needed to support other troops.

Finally, Bruce is even credited with using the 'wee folk' to charge at a crucial moment of the battle to demoralise the English. Whether that was part of Bruce's plan or not, we shall never know. Maybe luck does just go with winners.

How important was the battle of Bannockburn?

Victory at Bannockburn gave the Scots huge confidence – but so had victory at Stirling Bridge. So, did the battle achieve very much? Without doubt, the victory made Bruce's position as king of Scotland secure. He was a successful warlord and with military success comes more support.

The Scots also captured many English knights and they were used not only to earn ransoms but also in exchange for Scottish prisoners. In this way Bruce won back his wife, daughter and sister after almost ten years in captivity.

Finally, the aftermath of victory gave Bruce the time to stabilise and secure his authority over his kingdom.

However, the battle did not end the Scottish Wars of Independence. It did not force England to give Scotland its freedom and the battle did not significantly weaken English power.

The road to independence

Why did Bruce become known as 'Good King Robert' after Bannockburn?

Immediately after the battle of Bannockburn Bruce secured his position as king of Scots. For a long time Scottish nobles had been torn between their loyalty to the king of Scotland and their promises of loyalty to the English king to whom they did homage for the lands they held in England. Now Bruce decided it was time to settle the matter. The Scottish lords were given a stark decision – give up your lands in England and be rewarded by Bruce or keep your lands in England but lose all land and title in Scotland and forever be disinherited. At a parliament held at Cambuskenneth Abbey in November 1314 the new arrangements became law. The nobles who decided to keep their lands in England became known as 'the Disinherited' and bitterly resented what Bruce did to them. To Bruce and his supporters the action to stop the problem of divided loyalties made good political sense. Bruce had to be sure of his nobles' loyalty. Bruce rewarded those who now sided with him with land taken from the disinherited nobles and from Bruce's enemies who had died at Bannockburn.

Three years later, a Parliament held at Scone decided that if Robert did not produce an heir, his grandson Robert Stewart would become heir to the throne. If Robert Stewart was too young to be king then Thomas Randolph would act as Guardian, with Sir James, Lord of Douglas, as back-up if Randolph should die. Robert the Bruce had made sure that his kingdom did not suffer again from the problems that happened after the death of Alexander III.

By 1318, Bruce was secure in Scotland but the war with England continued. Soon after victory at Bannockburn, Bruce decided to take the war to Edward II in two ways. The first was to threaten English control in Ireland.

Why did Bruce send Scottish armies to fight in Ireland?

The Irish campaign made sense to Bruce. The English raised Irish levies to fight against the Scots. Ireland was also a base used by the English to launch attacks into Scotland. Finally, Bruce's brother, Edward, was ambitious and restless. A successful campaign in Ireland could result in Edward Bruce becoming king of Ireland!

At first the campaign seemed to be a success. The Irish lords seemed happy to see the Scots and in the summer of 1316 Edward Bruce was accepted as High King of Ireland.

Was the Irish campaign a failure?

Promises made are not the same as promises kept, and very soon the alliance of Irish lords fell apart, along with their promise to accept Edward Bruce as High King of Ireland. King Robert the Bruce had to travel in person to quell trouble in Ireland. The Scots only had limited success. They failed to capture Dublin and only managed to keep control over the northern part of Ireland called Ulster. Finally, the ambitions of the Bruce family in Ireland ended when Edward Bruce was killed.

Nevertheless, the Irish campaign had distracted English attention from Scotland and that was useful to Bruce. English forces that could have been used against Scotland or to protect northern England were diverted to deal with the trouble in Ireland. Edward II and his advisers could not plan campaigns against Scotland while they were more concerned about the possibility of a Celtic fringe alliance – in other words Scotland, Wales and Ireland uniting in common cause against the English.

Why did Bruce continue raids into northern England?

Over 100 years earlier Scottish kings had held an ambition to absorb the northern counties of England into Scotland. Whether Bruce really wanted to do that is unclear but his raids certainly caused trouble for King Edward II of England.

By 1318 Berwick had been recaptured and Scottish forces raided as far south as Newcastle. Edward II was forced to take action but Bruce seems to have guessed Edward's next moves. As a large English army lumbered north towards Berwick, a Scottish army avoided the enemy and raided southwards into Yorkshire. The Scots were dancing rings around Edward. While Edward laid siege to Berwick the Scots were ravaging his land in northern England.

Edward left Berwick in a vain attempt to catch the Scots raiders, but he failed. According to reports, the Scottish troops headed back north not because Edward was hunting for them but because they could not carry any more loot! Once again Bruce had humiliated the English king.

The Scottish raids continued. Once again Edward assembled an army and advanced into Scotland but once again, while near Edinburgh, the English force had to turn back because of lack of food.

It was increasingly obvious to the lords of northern England that Edward could do little to protect them and several made private arrangements with Bruce, mostly involving the payment of 'protection money'. One such person was the Earl of Carlisle. Edward was furious that his nobles in the north were making private deals with the Scots and the Earl of Carlisle was arrested and executed for treason – his crime being making a truce with the Scots. However, just a few months later Edward II did exactly the same thing and made a truce with Bruce that was to last for thirteen years.

By 1319, Edward II had been defeated in battle, his lands in the north of England were raided with ease by the Scots, his own nobles in the north were very unhappy with his kingship and Bruce had even threatened to open a Celtic alliance against him by invading Ireland. Edward II had even been forced to make a truce with Bruce. However, Edward would still not accept that Scotland was an independent nation, free from English expansionist ambitions.

What part did the Pope play in winning Scotland's independence?

A main issue that was central to the independence of Scotland was Bruce's right to be king. Remember that Bruce had committed a great sin by murdering John Comyn in a church. For that crime Bruce remained excommunicated although the Scots bishops had never enforced the excommunication on Bruce. In 1319 the Pope ordered Scotland's bishops to explain why they had never enforced the excommunication.

This was an opportunity Bruce turned to his benefit. Edward had tried to use international diplomacy to create pressure on Bruce. Now Bruce turned the tables on Edward and ordered three documents to be prepared for the Pope, each in their different ways justifying Bruce as king of Scotland. Two of the three have been lost to historians but the third, the Declaration of Arbroath, still survives.

Why is the Declaration of Arbroath so important?

Today, the words of the Declaration have many interpretations. Some say they are the first stirrings of a basic democracy in Europe, where kings could be removed if they displeased the people of the country. The Declaration stated, 'If he [Bruce] should agree to make our kingdom subject to the King of England, we should drive him out as our enemy'.

Are the words, 'for as long as a hundred remain alive we shall never on any conditions be brought under English rule' clear statements of national identity and pride in a nation?

Even the words, 'It is in truth not for glory, nor riches, nor honours that we are fighting, but for freedom' have been seen as a statement made by the Community of the Realm, making clear that their actions were carried out in the interests of the country as a whole rather than personal gain.

Another interpretation of the Declaration of Arbroath is that the words were just propaganda. Is the Declaration of Arbroath just a carefully worded document written on the orders of Bruce to justify his kingship and also to persuade the Pope to drop his opposition to Bruce as king of Scots? It is true that most of the Scots nobles who attached their seals to the document would never have read the document. However, the Declaration survives today as a truly important document that can legitimately be interpreted in all the ways outlined above.

Did the Declaration of Arbroath achieve Scottish freedom and independence?

In the short term it did not. Although the truce between England and Scotland limped along there was no formal making of peace between the two countries. Later negotiations with a new Pope in 1323 helped to ease relations between the Papacy and Scotland, but events in England were about to change the situation completely.

How important was the Soulis conspiracy of 1320?

Those nobles who had been disinherited were still bitter and others felt resentful of the power now wielded by the Bruce family. Nevertheless, the only evidence of discontent with Bruce as king of Scots after Bannockburn is an event described as the Soulis conspiracy. The conspirators were the remnants of discontented nobles who had not been promoted or rewarded by Bruce. Even Soulis himself had been an unsuccessful competitor for the crown. Bruce crushed the conspiracy easily and it was no real threat. The importance of the Soulis conspiracy is really only as a contrast to the Declaration of Arbroath. It reminds us that Bruce was not loved by all and the words of the Declaration of Arbroath were essentially pro-Bruce propaganda.

Why did England and Scotland eventually make peace?

After three years the truce between England and Scotland broke down. In England, discontent with Edward II's reign reached such a peak that in 1327 forces led by Isabella, his wife, and her lover, Mortimer, eventually overthrew him. Stories continue about the alleged horrific murder of Edward with a red-hot poker but, as far as Scotland was concerned, this was an opportunity not to be missed.

Bruce sent a Scottish army into northern England with the intention of putting pressure on Isabella, Mortimer and the new boy king, Edward III. Mortimer tried to defeat the Scots but under Sir James Douglas the Scots avoided battle and continued hit and run raids.

Bruce even began granting land in northern England to his followers. While these land grants were only made in name, since Bruce did not control the land, the symbolism of the action was obvious. English authority was so weak that perhaps Bruce would absorb the northern English counties into Scotland.

Meanwhile Bruce launched a new attack into Ireland, raiding into Ulster and raising English fears once again of a new Celtic alliance against England.

The pressure on Mortimer and Isabella's government was just too much. They agreed to negotiate with Bruce.

What were the Treaties of Edinburgh and Northampton?

The Treaty of Edinburgh was signed on 17 March 1328. Bruce gave up Scotland's claims to Northumbria and he agreed to pay compensation for damage caused totalling £20 000. In exchange, England accepted that Scotland was a free and independent country with Robert the Bruce as its officially recognised king. The matching Treaty of Northampton confirmed the Treaty of Edinburgh.

Three months later Bruce died, but he had lived long enough to see Scotland recognised as a free and independent nation with himself as the accepted king of Scots. Bruce knew his arrangements about who should be king after him (the succession) were secure and that the Bruce dynasty would continue.

The Wars of Independence, 1286–1328: a perspective

This final section will not be part of your exam. There will be no questions linked to it. However, to cover the syllabus you should be aware of the significance of the Wars of Independence in the development of Scottish identity.

The treaties of Edinburgh and Northampton did not end conflict between Scotland and England. Soon after the treaties were signed, the young Edward III tested his own ambitions by claiming the treaty agreed between Bruce and his mother did not bind him.

A pattern similar to before was re-established, with English invasion being met by Scottish counter-attack. However, the conflict between England and Scotland had become conflict between two separate countries, not one in which one country was trying to win its freedom and independence from the other.

Just over 250 years later, Scotland and England were united under one royal family with the Union of the Crowns in 1603. A hundred years after that, the Treaty of Union united the parliaments of the two countries in 1707.

Although Scotland became part of the union of Great Britain, Scotland never lost its identity and by the late 20th century the feeling that Scotland had its own strong spirit alive and well within the union of Great Britain led to devolution and the creation of Scotland's own Parliament.

Have the Wars of Independence any significance today?

Politically, the Wars of Independence are part of history but their emotional and national significance is still powerful. In economic terms the wars form the basis of a multi-million pound tourist industry. Emotionally, thousands of people lined the Royal Mile to welcome back the Stone of Destiny to Scotland in 1996. Such symbolism is so important that arrangements have been made to transport the stone to Westminster Abbey when it is required there for future coronation ceremonies.

Finally, the national symbolism of the Wars of Independence can be seen when Scots sing along with 'Flower of Scotland', Scotland's unofficial national anthem. The song reminds Scots directly of the struggle for independence against 'proud Edward' and how the Scots 'sent him homeward tae think again'.

Example question 1

Here is an example of a 'How useful ...' question, linked to Issue 3 of the Wars of Independence special topic.

Source A is a letter from Andrew Moray and William Wallace to the merchants of Lübeck, Germany, sent in October 1297.

> From Andrew of Moray and William Wallace, leaders of the army of the kingdom of Scotland, and of the community of the realm, to their beloved friends the mayors and common people of Lubeck and of Hamburg, greeting and increasing sincere affection.
>
> We have been told by trustworthy merchants of the kingdom of Scotland that you are considerate and helpful in all matters affecting us and our merchants and we are therefore more obliged to give you our thanks and a worthy repayment: to this end we willingly enter into an undertaking with you, asking you to have it announced to your merchants that they can have safe access to all ports of the Scottish kingdom with their merchandise, because the Kingdom of Scotland, thanks be to God, has been recovered by war from the power of the English.
>
> Fare well. Given at Haddington in Scotland, 11 October 1297

Question

How useful is source A as evidence of the importance of Wallace and Murray in the Scottish resistance against England? In reaching a conclusion you should refer to:

- the origin and possible purpose of the source
- the content of the source
- recalled knowledge
- use the following advice to help write a fluent answer.

Writing your answer

Use the following advice to help write a fluent answer.

- *Paragraph 1*
  Write about the **origin** and **purpose** of the source. Why does the fact that Wallace and Murray signed it make it more or less useful in terms of the question? Why do you think it was written (its purpose)? Why does the purpose help to make the source useful?
- *Paragraph 2*
  Refer to **one** point from the source and explain why it helps make the source useful. Develop the point made by using your own knowledge.
- *Paragraph 3*
  Refer to another point from the source and explain why it helps make the source useful. Develop the point made by using your own knowledge.
- *Paragraph 4*
  Finally, refer to a third piece of evidence from the source and explain why it helps make the source useful. Develop the point made by using your own knowledge.
- *Paragraph 5*
  Reach a final conclusion about how useful the source is. Mention the reasons that you think **do** make it useful then include any reasons you can think of that might limit the usefulness of the source. What you have done is reach a **balanced conclusion**.

How many marks would you give?

- Is there a direct comment on how the **origin** and **purpose** of the source help to make it useful? You can give **up to** 2 marks for doing that.
- Are there three different points taken from the source? Are the points developed (explained) and is it clear why these points help to make the source useful? You can give **up to** 2 marks for doing that.

- Is there some recall used either to develop points in the source or used in the balance section to suggest the source is not as useful as it could be? You can give **up to** 2 marks for doing that.

Example question 2

Here is an example of a comparison question, linked to Issue 4 of the Wars of Independence special topic. Remember that comparison questions can be used to test you on **any** of the issues. Look back to page 6 and read what you have to do to answer a comparison type question.

Source B is adapted from a recent textbook about the Battle of Bannockburn.

> The Scots won at Bannockburn because of careful planning. Bruce was unsure if a battle was really necessary and made his plans so that the Scots could vanish into the forests if necessary rather than face a large, confident and strong English army.
>
> Scottish control over the high road to Stirling was vital for victory and before the battle the Scots dug potts around the road to force the English to look for other ways to reach the castle. It soon became obvious that the only alternative route was across boggy ground unsuited to the English cavalry.
>
> On the other hand the Scots were well trained. The Scottish schiltrons were mobile and were used to attack as well as defend. By keeping the schiltrons pushing forward the Scots gave the English no room to move or to regroup. Bruce also knew how to use his cavalry as a force ready to react to any threat from English archers. Finally Bruce's leadership was vital. He is credited with using the 'small folk' to charge at a crucial moment of the battle, thereby demoralising the English.

Source C is from *A History of Military Defeats*.

> The English lost the battle of Bannockburn because of over-confidence and a poor leader. King Edward II lacked his father's skill and he added to the army's weaknesses by changing the chain of command and adding to confusion. Perhaps it was the confusion that led English commanders to make very odd decisions.
>
> The army was equipped with scouts who knew the landscape well. Why then did they suggest moving forces onto boggy land on which their room for manoeuvre was severely restricted by the Bannock burn and the Firth of Forth?
>
> When the battle began, the English cavalry advanced on the Scots expecting an easy victory. Why had they learned nothing from the errors of the first day of the battle or from their earlier victory at Falkirk? They knew that the way to deal with schiltrons was to use archers, defended by cavalry, and send wave after wave of arrows into the packed masses of Scots. So why did they not do that?
>
> We are left with the conclusion that the Battle of Bannockburn was not so much won by the Scots as lost by the English.

Question

To what extent do sources B and C agree in their opinions about why the Scots won the battle of Bannockburn? Compare the content overall and in detail.

Writing your answer

Use the following advice to help write a fluent answer.

- *Paragraph 1*
  Start by writing your overall comparison – do Sources B and C agree or disagree over why the Scots won at Bannockburn?
- *Paragraphs 2–5*:
  Deal with one detailed comparison in each paragraph. Find four points of comparison that the sources agree or disagree about. Explain each comparison fully by using brief quotes from the source and your own recalled knowledge.

How many marks would you give?

- Is there an overall comparison summing up the main difference between the sources? You can give a mark for that.
- Are there four more comparisons made and is each comparison well explained and not just a series of quotes from the sources? If the answer is yes then give 1 mark for each clear and correct comparison.

> **Top Tip**
> **Usually** in a comparison question you can gain marks for identifying and explaining points where the sources agree **and also** where they disagree. Don't always assume that the sources will take exactly opposite points of view. They might – but not always.

Example question 3

Here is an example of a 'How far...' question, linked to Issue 1 of the Wars of Independence study topic. Remember that 'How far...' questions can be used to assess **any** of the issues. Look back to page 6 and read what you have to do to answer a 'How far...' type question.

Source D is from a letter written by William Fraser, Bishop of St Andrews, to King Edward in 1290

> To Lord Edward, King of England from William, minister of the church of Saint Andrew in Scotland.
>
> There is a sorrowful rumour that our Lady Margaret of Norway is dead, on which account the kingdom of Scotland is disturbed and the community distracted. On hearing the rumour, Sir Robert de Bruce came with a great army to Perth but what he intends to do we know not. But the Earls of Mar and Atholl are already collecting their army and there is fear of a general war and a great slaughter of men.
>
> If it turns out that our Lady Margaret has departed this life, let your Excellency approach the border with an army to help save the shedding of blood and to set over Scotland a king who of right ought to have the succession, so long that he follows your advice. If Sir John Balliol comes to your presence we advise you to speak with him so that your honour and advantage be preserved.
>
> Given at Leuchars, in the year of our Lord, 1290.

Question

How far does source D help us to understand the difficulties facing Scotland caused by the death of Alexander III?

Writing your answer

Use the following advice to help write a fluent answer.

The source comments on examples of difficulties facing Scotland caused by the death of Alexander III such as the royal succession and Margaret's death, ambitious nobles and the risk of civil war, the request for help from Edward. Write a brief paragraph on each of the difficulties mentioned in the source. Try to use your own knowledge to explain (perhaps with quotes) why those points were difficulties facing Scotland or would lead to difficulties. For example, you could explain exactly why the death of Alexander led to a crisis in the royal succession and why Margaret's death made the situation so much worse.

You should then use your own knowledge to write about other difficulties facing Scotland as a direct result of the death of Alexander.

How many marks would you give?

- Does your answer clearly select from the source four different difficulties facing Scotland caused by the death of Alexander III? You can give **up to** 4 marks for doing that.
- Does your answer provide balance by using a lot of recall about other difficulties facing Scotland? You can give **up to** 7 marks for that.

Example question 4

Here is an example of a 'How fully...' question, linked to Issue 2 of the Wars of Independence study topic. Remember that 'How fully...' questions, like all the other question types, can be used to assess **any** of the issues. Look back to page 6 and read what you have to do to answer a 'How fully...' type question.

Source E is from a letter issued by King John at Kincardine or Brechin, July 1296.

> John, by the grace of God, king of Scotland, greets all who shall see or hear this letter.
>
> In view of the fact that through bad and wrong advice and our own foolishness we have in many ways gravely displeased and angered our lord Edward, king of England, in that while we still owed him fealty and homage we made an alliance with the king of France against him ... we have defied our lord the king of England and have withdrawn ourselves from his homage and fealty by renouncing our homage ... we have sent our men into his land of England to burn, loot, murder and commit other wrongs and have fortified the land of Scotland against him ... for all these reasons the king of England entered the realm of Scotland and conquered it by force despite the army we sent against him, something he had a right to do as lord of his fee.
>
> Therefore acting of our own free will we have surrendered the land of Scotland and all of its people with the homage of them all due to him.

Question

How fully does source E explain the relationship between John Balliol and Edward I?
Use the source and recalled knowledge.

Writing your answer

Use the following advice to help write a fluent answer.

The source comments on the relationship between John Balliol and Edward I by using examples such as Balliol breaking his oath of loyalty to Edward, the Scottish treaty with France, war between Scotland and England, and the Scottish surrender.

Write a brief paragraph on each of the points about the relationship mentioned in the source. Try to use your own knowledge to explain (perhaps with quotes) the issues involved in the relationship between Balliol and Edward. For example, you could explore more fully the issues of fealty, homage and feudal overlordship.

You should then use your own knowledge to write more about the relationship between Edward and Balliol.

How many marks would you give?

- Does the answer select information from the source and explain it briefly? You can give **up to** 4 marks for doing that.
- Does your answer provide a balance to the answer by using a lot of recall that is relevant to the question? You can give **up to** 7 marks for that.

When researching history topics for yourself, we recommend looking at the following websites:

- SCRAN (*www.scran.ac.uk*), a website run by the Royal Commission on the Ancient and Historical Monuments of Scotland, containing over 360,000 images and documents from museums and archives.
- Learning and Teaching Scotland's website (*www.ltscotland.org.uk/higherscottishhistory*), which has sections on all the units of Higher History.

The Treaty of Union, 1689–1740: the background

This section is about what Scotland was like in the years just before union with England in 1707.

Issue 1 – Worsening relations with England

This issue is about why the relationship between England and Scotland worsened in the 1690s and early 1700s.

Issue 2 – Arguments for and against union with England

This issue is about arguments for and against a union between Scotland and England.

Issue 3 – The passing of the Act of Union

This issue is about how the Act of Union took place.

Issue 4 – The effects of the union, to 1740

This issue is about how the union affected Scotland up to 1740.

The Treaty of Union, 1689–1740: a perspective

This section provides an opportunity to reflect on the union and its effects on the development of Scottish identity.

The Treaty of Union, 1689–1740: the background

This section is about what Scotland was like in the years just before union with England in 1707.

To cover the syllabus you should know about the following:

- What the Revolution Settlement of 1688–89 means.
- How the Revolution Settlement affected the Church and government of Scotland.
- In what ways Scotland was a divided and tense society before union.
- How Scotland was politically 'managed' before union.

Why does this course start in 1689?

In 1689 changes happened that were to affect Scotland and the rest of the UK right up until today. The first change involved a husband and wife called William and Mary being invited to seize the throne from King James VII and II. He was the seventh King James of Scotland so he was James VII of Scotland. The same James was also king of England but as he was only the second King James of England he was called James VII and II.

This change in monarch was called the Glorious Revolution in England, while in Scotland it was referred to as the Revolution Settlement.

The Revolution Settlement

Who was James VII and II?

Since 1603 and the Union of the Crowns, Scotland and England had shared the same king and queen. Kings of Scotland from the Stuart family became kings of Britain. When the Union of the Crowns took place James VI of Scotland became also James I of England. After James came Charles I and then, after a short break when Britain had no king during the rule of Oliver Cromwell, the monarchy was restored in 1660 and Charles II became king. Charles II was succeeded in 1685 by another James – James the VII and II – but suddenly there was a problem. James VII and II was a Roman Catholic!

Why was King James' Roman Catholicism a problem?

Since the Union of the Crowns all the kings had been Protestant. England and Scotland were officially Protestant countries. However, when James VII and II became king he started to promote other Roman Catholics to top jobs. James promoted Roman Catholic army officers and he filled Parliament with his supporters.

Roman Catholics were allowed to worship free from persecution, and powerful Protestants in England and Scotland began to worry that Roman Catholic power in Britain would grow. Protestant politicians in England felt that an increase in Roman Catholic power could hurt Protestant England and in particular it might threaten the power of Parliament. Only a few years before, the English Civil War had been fought mainly over the issue of who had most power – the Crown or Parliament. Since then Parliament had jealously guarded its power. Would King James try to restrict that power?

James VII and II

King James was an old man and next in line was his daughter, Mary, who was Protestant and married to a Dutch prince called William of Orange. It was thought that when James died Protestant power would be safe but in July 1688 James' wife had a son and James announced that his son and heir would be raised as a Roman Catholic. The English Protestant Church (called the Anglican Church) feared the rise of Roman Catholic power in Britain. Something had to be done, and what was done was called 'The Glorious Revolution'.

What happened in the Glorious Revolution?

James VII and II's daughter was called Mary. She was Protestant and had married William of Orange. The House of Orange was the name of the royal family in the Netherlands.

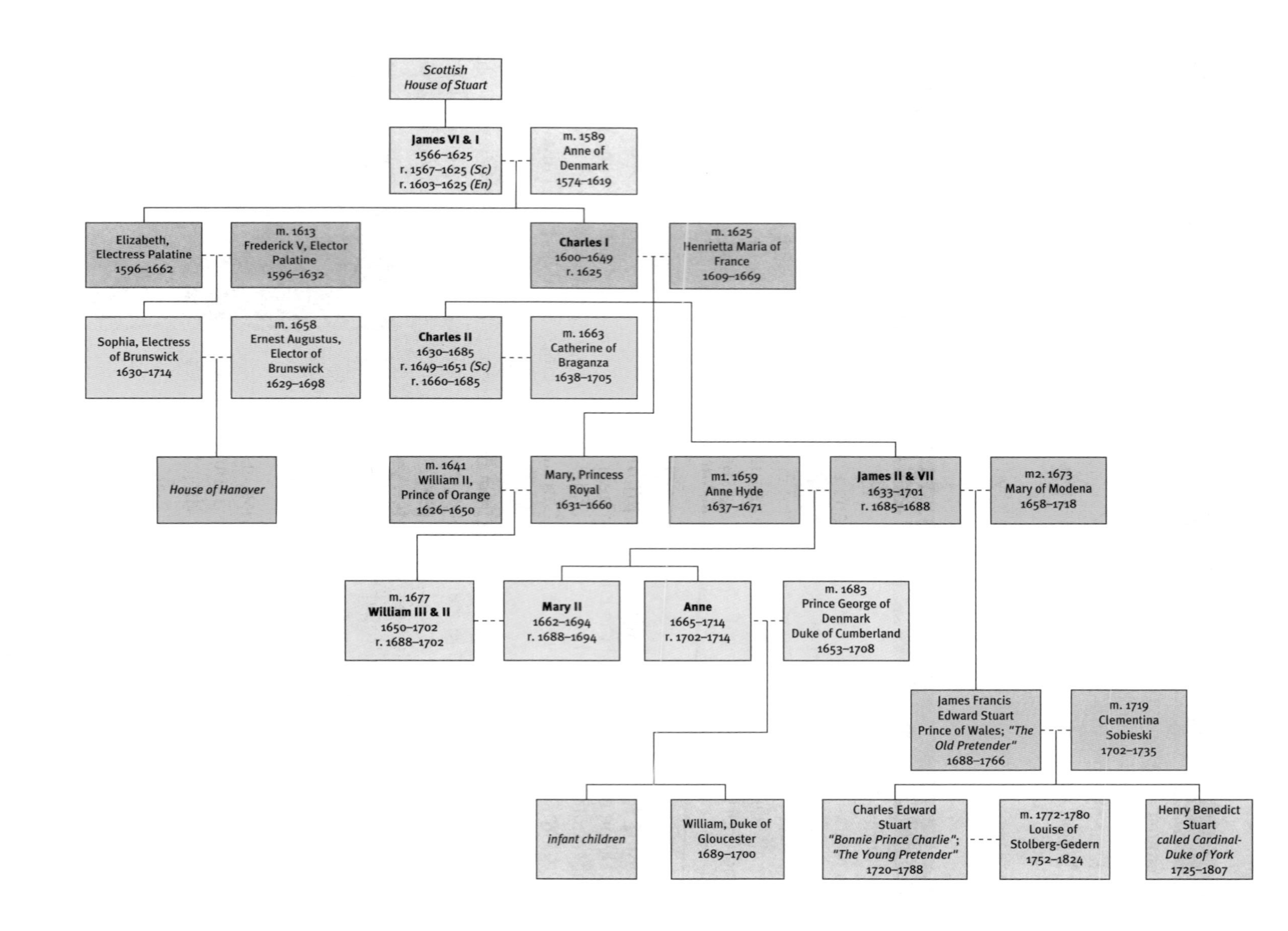
Scottish House of Stuart
James VI & I 1566–1625 r. 1567–1625 (Sc) r. 1603–1625 (En)
m. 1589 Anne of Denmark 1574–1619
Elizabeth, Electress Palatine 1596–1662
m. 1613 Frederick V, Elector Palatine 1596–1632
Charles I 1600–1649 r. 1625
m. 1625 Henrietta Maria of France 1609–1669
Sophia, Electress of Brunswick 1630–1714
m. 1658 Ernest Augustus, Elector of Brunswick 1629–1698
Charles II 1630–1685 r. 1649–1651 (Sc) r. 1660–1685
m. 1663 Catherine of Braganza 1638–1705
House of Hanover
m. 1641 William II, Prince of Orange 1626–1650
Mary, Princess Royal 1631–1660
m1. 1659 Anne Hyde 1637–1671
James II & VII 1633–1701 r. 1685–1688
m2. 1673 Mary of Modena 1658–1718
m. 1677 William III & II 1650–1702 r. 1688–1702
Mary II 1662–1694 r. 1688–1694
Anne 1665–1714 r. 1702–1714
m. 1683 Prince George of Denmark Duke of Cumberland 1653–1708
James Francis Edward Stuart Prince of Wales; "The Old Pretender" 1688–1766
m. 1719 Clementina Sobieski 1702–1735
infant children
William, Duke of Gloucester 1689–1700
Charles Edward Stuart "Bonnie Prince Charlie"; "The Young Pretender" 1720–1788
m. 1772-1780 Louise of Stolberg-Gedern 1752–1824
Henry Benedict Stuart called Cardinal-Duke of York 1725–1807

Protestant groups in England encouraged William to land in England and overthrow James. It was risky, but William thought it well worth the risk. British supporters of William argued it was a move to protect Parliament and the Protestant religion. For William it was a chance to increase his power in Europe. William was ambitious and saw France as a potential enemy. By accepting the invitation to become king in Britain, it could mean Britain might help William in a war against Roman Catholic France.

On 5 November 1688 William landed in England at the head of a Dutch army. Eventually James fled to France and the English Parliament declared that James had abdicated and so given up his right to be king. Originally the plan had been for Mary, James' daughter, to become queen in her own right. However, William insisted on being made king, so on 13 February 1689 the joint reign of William and Mary began. Within five years Mary had died and William was left as king of Britain to rule on his own.

The name 'Glorious Revolution' sounds wonderful. In fact, it was a description created by William's propaganda machine. Basically, it was a deal between the English Parliament and William of Orange.

- Parliament argued that since James had run away to France he had effectively given up the throne of Britain.
- William and his wife Mary were offered the roles of king and queen.
- Parliament would support the war against France, while William and Mary would accept new limits on their authority as king and queen of Britain.
- Parliament was happy that the power of the monarchy had been restricted and also that a Protestant monarchy had been secured.

That was the Glorious Revolution – at least that is the English version! The situation was rather different in Scotland.

Scotland in 1689

Scotland in 1689 was poor and its population was small, only about 1 million people (just one-fifth of today's total). The biggest town was Edinburgh but its population was only 30 000, about the size of present-day Dalkeith, Ardrossan or Dumfries. Glasgow had not yet developed into a city based on trade and industry. It was a small town on the Clyde, about the size of present-day Haddington.

Travelling within Scotland was difficult and dangerous. As a result of the poor road network, the easiest way to travel was by sea, and most of Scotland's trade was with northern Europe. As a result the richest places in Scotland were the trading towns (the burghs) on Scotland's east coast such as Leith, Perth and even Crail!

England was also difficult to get to. Apart from a coast road along the line of the present-day A1 to Berwick upon Tweed, Scotland had no easy route to England. The border hills and rivers isolated Scotland.

Since 1603 and the Union of the Crowns, Scotland and England had shared the same king, but Scotland and England had different laws and different parliaments.

Scotland in 1689 was in many ways a divided country. Divisions within the country included:

- divisions between towns (burghs) and countryside
- divisions between landowners and businessmen
- divisions between Highlands and Lowlands
- divisions between Presbyterians and Episcopalians.

This all made Scotland a divided nation and a very different country from England.

How was Scotland divided over religion?

Scotland was a Protestant country. That means that most Scots followed a form of worship within the Christian Church which was very different from the Roman Catholic tradition. In fact, the name Protestant comes from people who protested about things they did not like in the Roman Catholic Church. Although England was also Protestant, Church organisation differed greatly between England and Scotland. For example, in England the king could choose the bishops who ran the Church of England.

In 1662 Charles II tried to do the same in Scotland but Scottish Protestants (called Presbyterians) were against the use of bishops. They believed that each local congregation should choose its own ministers and that these ministers would manage their Churches through local committees called presbyteries. In effect, Presbyterians (that is, most Scots) wanted the Church to look after itself by means of its own 'parliament': the General Assembly. Presbyterians did not want any interference from the king.

How was Scotland divided by geography?

Scotland was divided into two different areas – the Highlands and the Lowlands. About half of all Scots lived north of Perth in scattered farms and villages. They survived on farming and the cattle trade. Much of Highland society was divided into clans, a clan chief having total loyalty from clansmen and clansmen having a duty to fight for their clan chief when called to do so. In the Lowlands, local power was in the hands of landowners known as lairds. The more land that was owned by a laird, the more power that laird had. Smaller landowners hoped to make marriage connections with the important land-owning families of Scotland or in some other way become linked to them. That way, powerful friends could lead to wealth and political power.

Highland society was very different from Lowland society, with language and religion being two main areas of difference. In the Highlands, Gaelic was the language usually spoken, and Roman Catholics and Episcopalians were more common here than in Lowland Scotland.

Episcopalianism was in many ways a combination of Roman Catholic and Anglican practices and Episcopalians disagreed most strongly with Presbyterians. Episcopalians accepted the authority of bishops, so disagreements between Episcopalians and Presbyterians were the cause of a major division within Scottish society.

How did the Scottish Parliament operate?

Political power was in the hands of the king and his Commissioners. A Commissioner was another name for what we would call today an MSP – a Member of the Scottish Parliament.

In the Scottish Parliament the Three Estates sat together. (It might be helpful to think of an estate as a social class.) The First Estate was the clergy (Church leaders), the Second Estate was the nobility of Scotland (the earls, dukes and so on) and the Third Estate was made up burgesses, merchants from Scotland's royal burghs, which were towns with special trading rights.

The Scottish Parliament sat in one long room. On one side of the room sat the Commissioners from the countryside, on the other sat the Commissioners from the burghs. In the middle sat the clerks, the Constable and the Marshal, who managed and recorded the daily business.

However, do not think that Parliament was anything like it is today. The Scottish Parliament could **not** pass laws. It could **not** even discuss and debate new laws proposed by the king. Ordinary people did **not** elect the Commissioners. What Parliament **did** do was arrange the raising of money to pay for wars and present the illusion that the Commissioners really were the community of Scotland and that they agreed with what the king wanted to do.

The Commissioners and landowners who bothered to attend Parliament knew that their future progress and wealth depended on not offending the king. James VI and I even wrote from his throne in London, 'Here I sit and govern Scotland with my pen. I write and it is done.' In practice, James and other kings appointed a Privy Council to rule Scotland on the king's behalf. In reality, the Scottish Parliament had almost no power at all over the king.

Did Scotland welcome William and Mary?

The Scottish Parliament had to decide whether to accept William and his wife Mary as the new king and queen. Opinion in Scotland was divided between whether to support King James or King William. Scottish Protestants were unhappy about the reign of Roman Catholic James but were also suspicious about William.

In April 1689 representatives of the Scottish counties and burghs, along with some powerful nobles, met in a Convention to reach a decision about who to support. Both William and James sent letters to the Scottish Parliament hoping to influence their decision. William made

William and Mary

it easier for the Scots to choose him because he promised to defend the Protestant faith and seemed to promise to leave the General Assembly to continue to manage the Church of Scotland as it saw fit. In his letter to the Scottish Parliament, William wrote about the importance of securing the Protestant religion, whereas James' letter to the Scottish Parliament was more threatening.

Many historians argue that there was never really any doubt that Parliament would choose William. If Scotland had chosen James, a war might have broken out with England and Scottish Presbyterians would never have chosen Roman Catholic James as their king.

How did the Scottish Parliament increase its authority?

William needed to make sure that Scotland did not pose any problems during his war in Europe against Louis XIV's France. That was a main reason why he agreed to a Presbyterian settlement of the Scottish Church in 1690. In return, the Scottish Parliament granted William twenty-eight months of funding for his war against the French.

The Scottish Parliament also knew that William needed it more than it needed him, so the Parliament said they would only accept William as king if he agreed to certain conditions. These conditions were to protect the independence of the Protestant Church, limit the powers of the king and increase the powers of the Parliament.

On 11 April 1689, the Scottish Parliament produced the Claim of Right. This document offered the Crown to William and Mary and stated that James had 'forfeited' the Crown as a result of his behaviour. The Claim of Right was followed rapidly by another document called the Articles of Grievance. This document was the point where the Scottish Parliament seemed to assert its independence and its power. The Articles of Grievance aimed to end the king's control over the Scottish Parliament. The Scottish Parliament wanted to have complete freedom to discuss what it thought necessary, and not just follow the king's orders.

William and Mary reluctantly accepted both documents. William was not happy about the deal but he needed money and soldiers from both Scotland and England to help in his war with France. By agreeing to the conditions laid down by the Scottish Parliament William and Mary were accepted as the new king and queen of Scotland.

Were William and Mary popular in Scotland?

For Lowland Protestant Scots, William and Mary were acceptable. Mary was the daughter of the former King James and so the royal family line of the Stuarts was continued. The Kirk (as the presbyterian Church of Scotland was called) was also content to accept the new monarchs now that promises had been given to protect the Protestant religion. After all, Queen Mary was not only part of the royal family line but also she was Protestant. As far as the Scottish Parliament was concerned, its power had increased by the promises it had won from William and Mary.

However, there were other groups who were **not** happy with the reign of William and Mary. The largest of those groups were the Jacobites.

The Jacobites

Who were the Jacobites?

Jacobites were people who wanted to put James VII and II back on to the British throne. The Latin for James is Jacobus, and so the supporters of James VII and II were called Jacobites.

As soon as the Scottish Parliament chose William and Mary as the new king and queen of Britain, Jacobites started to gather their forces. In 1689 the first Jacobite rebellion against the British Crown took place.

Many of the Jacobite supporters came from the Highlands, where many clans were either Episcopalian or Roman Catholic. They had no love for the Presbyterian form of worship that William had promised to protect. It has been thought that some clans also supported the Jacobites out of old clan rivalry. Since William's authority in the Highlands was enforced by the Clan Campbell, other clans who hated the Campbells would automatically become Jacobite! However, several historians now doubt that reason for Jacobite support. What they do agree on is that the most likely reason for Jacobite support was simply that Jacobites believed they were fighting for the rightful king of Scotland. James was a member of the Stuart family and that family had been the unquestioned kings of Scotland for hundreds of years.

What did the Jacobites do in 1689?

At first Jacobite supporters brought their armed men into Edinburgh to try to persuade Parliament to reject William as king. When Parliament ignored Jacobite pressure the Jacobites left the city, led by James Graham, Viscount Claverhouse. They moved north and prepared to fight. On 27 July 1689 the Jacobite army faced King William's government army at Killiecrankie. Although the Jacobites were outnumbered almost 2:1 they had the advantage of the high ground, and when the wild Highlanders charged down the hillside the inexperienced government troops broke and ran. It seemed as if the Jacobites might march on Edinburgh but in the battle Claverhouse, the Jacobite leader, had been shot and killed.

Without their leader, the Jacobite army was forced to withdraw from Dunkeld on 21 August 1689 by a government force and then it was finally defeated at the Haughs of Cromdale on 1 May 1690. The defeat marked the end of the first Jacobite Rebellion – but the threat of Jacobitism continued and William's Scottish government knew that the Jacobite threat had to be kept at bay. (This helps to explain why the Massacre of Glencoe, 1692, was ordered – see pages 49–51)

What was the importance of the Jacobite rebellion of 1689?

First of all, the rebellion alerted William and England to the danger of leaving Scotland uncontrolled. Remember that William was also the military commander of the Netherlands, and which were involved in wars against Roman Catholic France and Spain. What would happen if Jacobites won support from those Roman Catholic countries that saw Scotland as a base from which to attack England?

Secondly, the Jacobite rebellion alerted Presbyterian Scots to the dangers of a return of King James. If James returned as king he would re-establish Roman Catholicism in Scotland. The Scottish Presbyterian Church would be threatened.

Finally, Parliament was also concerned that the return of a Stuart king would weaken its power. Stuart kings believed they were chosen by God and had a 'divine right' to rule, yet the Scottish Parliament had only just gained new powers over the monarchy. It did not want to lose its new powers to a returning Stuart king.

Is there a connection between the Jacobites and growing support for a political union between Scotland and England?

Yes, there is. Throughout William's reign he was concerned that Jacobites could use Scotland as a base from which to attack England. Politicians in both Scotland and England began to see advantages in a full union between the countries. A union could help preserve Protestant Presbyterianism in Scotland; it would maintain the power of Parliament over the Crown, and it would shut the door to any threats of war between Scotland and England.

Issue 1 – Worsening relations with England

This issue is about what happened in the 1690s and early 1700s to make relations between England and Scotland even worse.

To cover the syllabus you should know about the following:

- How England's foreign wars and the Navigation Acts made relations between England and Scotland worse.
- How the Darien Scheme made Scotland's economic problems worse.
- How other incidents such as the Glencoe massacre made relations worse.
- What the issue of the succession was and how it increased tension between Scotland and England.

The difficulties faced by Scotland in the 1690s were often blamed on King William. In fact, those who disliked William referred to a period in the 1690s as 'King William's seven ill years'. Natural disasters such as seven wet summers in a row led to real famine and starvation in Scotland. People were reported falling down dead in the street and babies died from starvation, as their mothers had no milk to feed them with.

At the same time the poor state of the Scottish economy had slashed the value of the Scottish currency. At one time an English pound and a Scots pound were equal in value. By the 1690s the Scots pound was only worth one-twelfth of the English pound. The result was that everything that had to be brought into Scotland was hugely expensive. The result of that was that the poor continued to starve.

The Union of the Crowns in 1603 had certainly weakened Scotland's economy. Now that the kings of Britain were in London, all the top jobs had also drifted to London. Edinburgh had lost huge amounts of business and Scotland was in decline. The king seldom, if ever, visited and it seemed as if Scotland had been forgotten about. Scotland's economy slumped.

By the 1690s long-term problems from before the arrival of William and Mary, such as increased poverty and an economy going into decline, were blamed on the new monarchs. However, there were other events in the Scotland of the 1690s that led to worsening relations with England.

What was the Massacre of Glencoe?

The events in Glencoe on 13 February 1692 further worsened relations between Scotland and England. Many people in Scotland felt that King William was directly involved in the Massacre of Glencoe in which thirty-eight MacDonalds who lived in Glencoe were murdered and the rest of the clan were left scattered in a blizzard, fearing for their lives.

Why was King William concerned about the Highlands of Scotland?

Ever since the Jacobite Rebellion in 1689 King William had suspected that the Highlands were a potential threat to the political stability of Scotland and perhaps even a threat to his throne. William knew that Episcopalian and Roman Catholic clans could easily have supported a Jacobite fightback. William also knew that France, now at war with William's Britain, might also support a Jacobite rising.

Glencoe

If William was distracted by a second war against the clans in Scotland, it would be much more difficult to fight the French at the same time. It was also possible that the French could supply and support a Jacobite rising and even

The Treaty of Union, 1689–1740

invade England through its northern border with Scotland. Quite simply, the clans had to be brought under control.

What was the background to the massacre?

In 1691 all Highland chiefs were told they must swear an oath of loyalty to King William by the end of the year. The problem was that the clan chiefs had already sworn loyalty to James. To the clan chiefs such a promise of loyalty was almost physically binding. The clan chiefs were torn between practical reality and their consciences. At the last moment, with only days to go before the end-of-year deadline, James released them from their oaths to him. In fact Maclain, the clan chief of the MacDonalds of Glencoe, only found out on 30 December 1691 that James VII and II had freed him from his oath. Faced with an impossible deadline, the chief set off through a snowstorm and reached Fort William the same day. He was then told that the oath could only be taken at Inveraray, nearly 75 miles away.

Eventually Maclain of Glencoe took the oath five days late. Maclain was told his oath would be accepted but behind the scenes other issues came into play.

Why did the massacre happen?

Sir John Dalrymple, the Earl of Stair, was heavily involved in the plans for the massacre of Glencoe. It was said that Dalrymple wanted to make an example of a 'disloyal' clan and the MacDonalds of Glencoe certainly 'fitted the frame' of a clan that could be made an example of. The chief was Roman Catholic. He was known to be a Jacobite and, after all, he had missed the deadline, swearing to be loyal five days too late.

Dalrymple was also ambitious. King William was an absentee king of Scotland. He took little interest in Scottish affairs and it is more than likely that ambitious Scottish politicians such as Dalrymple saw a way to increase their own reputation by demonstrating their efficiency and loyalty to the Crown. Dalrymple, then, expected King William to show his gratitude with titles and promotions.

Was the massacre deliberately planned?

The massacre was planned to the last detail. By 23 January 1692, Sir Thomas Livingstone, commander of the government's troops in Scotland, had ordered the commander at Fort William 'not to trouble the government with prisoners' from Glencoe.

Other orders followed, 'to fall upon the rebels of the MacDonalds of Glencoe, and put all to the sword under 70'. Captain Robert Campbell was officer in charge of the soldiers who marched into Glencoe. He knew that if he wanted to keep his job he had to carry out his orders.

What happened in Glencoe on 13 February 1692?

A company of government soldiers had stayed with the MacDonalds as guests. The MacDonalds believed that the soldiers had come to collect taxes. Highland hospitality meant that any group of people travelling, especially in winter, would be offered shelter and food. For twelve days the government troops lived as guests and friends of the MacDonalds. Then, on 13 February 1692, the soldiers attacked the clansmen in their beds. Men, women and children were slaughtered or left to run into the mountains and die in the snow. Many did survive, but thirty-eight did not.

How did the Massacre of Glencoe become an international news event?

Violence and murder were nothing new in the Highlands. Atrocities had been carried out between clans for generations. However, in this case, the events had political importance to the opponents of William. It is claimed that news of the scandal of the massacre broke when Captain Campbell, officer in charge, lost a copy of his orders when drunk in Edinburgh. Why he had a copy in his pocket after the event and how they were lost is unclear. What is completely clear is that the copy of the orders to Captain Campbell was used by Jacobites to discredit William and his government in Scotland. The Jacobites produced propaganda pamphlets mixing fact with allegation to condemn William's policy in Scotland.

Why did the Massacre of Glencoe have serious consequences for William and his government?

The problem for King William was that the events of Glencoe became national and international news. All of Scotland, even Lowlanders who had no reason to like Highlanders, was outraged. The bare facts of the massacre were developed and exaggerated with descriptions of children being stabbed as they begged for mercy and of rings being bitten from women's fingers by the soldiers.

King William and his Scottish government were condemned for betraying the trust of hosts who had offered hospitality. Under Scots law, that was a criminal offence called 'slaughter under trust'.

News of the massacre gave new life to the Jacobite cause. The whole scandal seemed to demonstrate William's lack of real concern for Scottish affairs.

Was William guilty of involvement in the massacre?

The finger of blame was pointed at William as the 'man behind the plan' but no one ever stood trial. The official enquiry in 1695 blamed the Earl of Stair and various military officers for the massacre but there was no firm evidence that William ordered the massacre. In Scottish legal terms, the king's guilt was 'not proven'. Later, it was claimed that Dalrymple wrote the order to 'extirpate [wipe out] that sect of thieves' but the king's signature also appeared twice on the order. There was no doubt the 'sect of thieves' referred to was the MacDonald clan of Glencoe.

The Massacre of Glencoe was a scandal that soured relations between Scotland and England, not least because there was a considerable suspicion that the investigation into the scandal had been a 'whitewash' that allowed William and his government to escape justice.

Trade and colonies

Scots were envious of England's colonies and tried many ways to make trade links with them. Such links were banned under the Navigation Acts. In the 1690s, King William's actions to enforce the Navigation Acts became one more part of the worsening relations with England.

What were the Navigation Acts?

In the 1660s England had passed Navigation Acts to protect English trade. These laws stated that all cargo carried to or from English colonies had to be carried on English ships with English crews. They also stated that all trade with English colonies had to come and go only from English ports. The Navigation Acts were designed to benefit England only and certainly excluded Scotland from benefiting from English trade wealth.

Why were colonies and trade such big issues in the 1690s?

By the late 17th century many European countries were becoming rich from the proceeds of foreign trade. Some countries, such as England and Spain, even colonised, or took over, other parts of the world and exploited those areas for their own profits. In Asia, Africa and increasingly the Americas European traders were developing trade routes and making more and more money for their home countries. Meanwhile in Scotland the late 17th century were years of economic decline and disaster. The Scottish Parliament decided that the best way to improve the economy would be to encourage international trade.

Why did the issues of trade and the colonies make relations between Scotland and England worse?

Scotland began to look at England's international trade with envy. Many Scots who had emigrated to English colonies reported on the wealth that was generated there. Scottish smugglers and illegal traders were making fortunes from trade with England's colonies.

As England became wealthier from trade with its colonies Scots began to argue that they should also be allowed to share in trade with England's colonies. After all, they argued, were not Scotland and England united under one king? The Scots also argued that they had lost France as a trading partner. When William became king he took Britain to war against France. Scotland could now no longer trade easily with its old ally and long-term trading partner.

English businessmen did not agree with Scotland's point of view! They guarded their trade routes jealously and were unwilling to let other countries 'muscle in' on their territories and colonies.

Nevertheless the Scots still tried to find ways around the Navigation Acts, often simply by ignoring them, or by forging documents and bribing officials. By the 1680s it was proving very hard to make the Navigation Acts work and from the English point of view the Scots were stealing from England's trading wealth.

After William became king he put English interests first and clamped down on the Scots operating within the 'English Empire'. Previously, King James VII and II had tried to encourage Scottish interests. He had allowed Scots to become involved in the English-controlled Royal Africa Company and the Hudson Bay Company in Canada. Now, under William, all that stopped. The Scots were furious and began to look elsewhere to develop their trade. The tensions over colonies and trade between England and Scotland were at the root of what became known as the Darien Disaster.

What was the Darien Scheme?

In the 1690s Scotland tried to set up a colony at Darien, on a fairly narrow strip of land in Central America between North and South America. It was about 50 miles wide. On the east coast of Darien was the Atlantic Ocean. On the west coast was the Pacific Ocean. If the Scots could operate an overland route between the coasts they would make a fortune by providing a service that would shorten the trading routes between Europe and Asia.

It was a reasonable idea. Today the same basic idea operates as the Panama Canal – a vital trade link between the Atlantic and Pacific. However, the 17th-century plan failed and some Scots blamed that failure on a lack of English support – although the Scots themselves really had to take the blame for the failure of the plan. The whole event became known as the Darien Disaster and almost bankrupted Scotland.

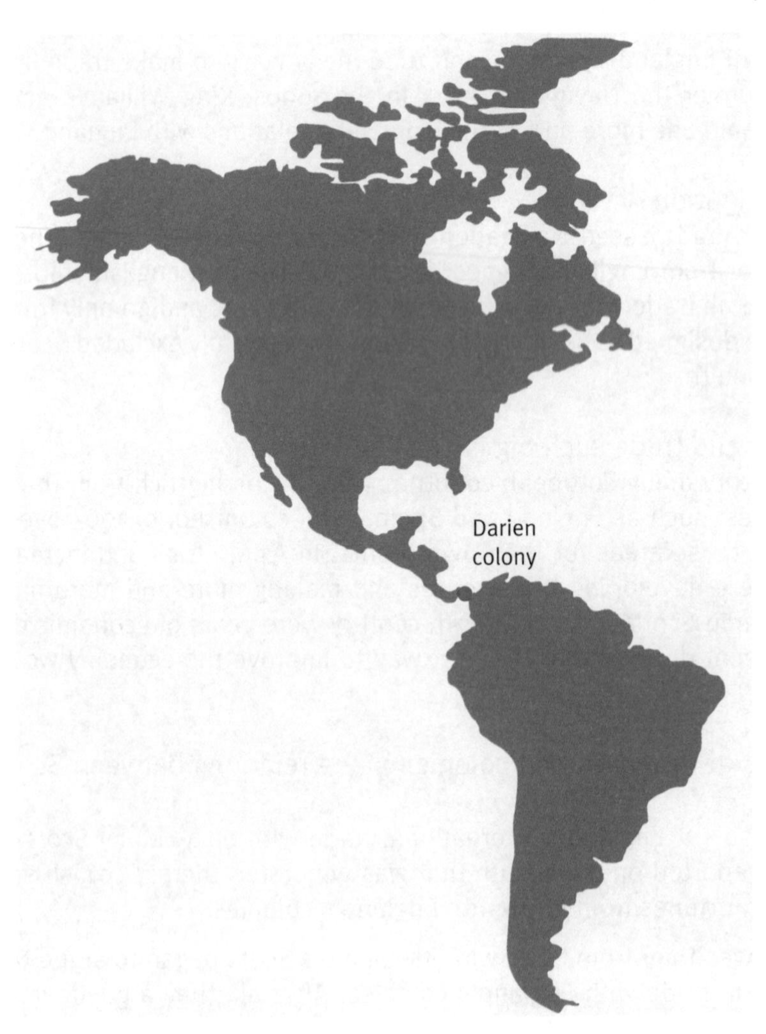

Location of Darien

To understand the Darien Scheme, we have to go back to 1693, when the Scottish Parliament passed an Act that allowed Scottish merchants to form companies to trade in all parts of the world where the king was not at war. English traders protested that this would lead to trading competition but for once William took the side of the Scots. William was well aware of his unpopularity in Scotland. The Jacobite rebellion of 1689 had shown William the possibility and dangers of an unsettled Scotland and news of the massacre at Glencoe had made William even more unpopular. Politically, it made sense to William to let the Scots have their way over boosting their trade.

What was the Company of Scotland?

In 1695 William Paterson (who had founded the Bank of England), along with several other Scottish merchants, set up the Company of Scotland with the power to 'to navigate their own or hired ships to any lands in Asia, Africa or America, there to plant [establish] colonies and the company shall have the absolute right to all manner of treasures profits, riches etc'. It all sounded too good to be true and it was!

The new Company of Scotland had a monopoly of Scottish trade with Africa and Asia forever and a thirty-one-year monopoly of trade with America. Investors rushed to join and the Company hoped to raise the huge sum of £600 000 by selling shares. Half were reserved for Scots; English investors bought up the other half within days. The Company of Scotland was off to a good start.

How did the English Parliament damage the Company of Scotland?

The English Parliament soon became worried about possible competition from the Scots so it did everything in its power to weaken the new Company of Scotland. The English Parliament accused any English person who had invested in the Company of Scotland of committing a serious crime against English interests and almost overnight English investors became scared and withdrew their money from the Company.

To further weaken the new Scottish Company, the English Parliament also wrote to every English colony forbidding them to trade with or give any help to the new Scottish Company. Finally the English Parliament also threatened to remove trading rights and profits from any **foreign** port or country that tried to work with Scotland. For example, England threatened to take their trade in cotton away from Hamburg if the German traders tried to invest in the Company of Scotland.

It was clear that the English Parliament was determined to ruin the Company of Scotland.

The Company of Scotland was left to struggle on alone. It raised £400 000 from Scottish investors and some historians believe that was half of all the money in Scotland at that time. Scotland was running a huge risk with the plan to trade internationally.

Why did Scots support the Darien Scheme?

By mid-1695 it was clear many Scottish investors were unwilling to run the risk of going anywhere near English colonies for fear English ships might attack them. As a result, the Scots decided to support the idea of William Paterson. His plan was known as the Darien Scheme.

Paterson claimed that Darien was the economic 'key to the universe'. Later historians think he based his claims on stories from a pirate who said Darien **'possibly'** had gold and that the natives were **'perhaps'** friendly. In reality, the Scots had no idea what Darien was like. It was tropical rainforest with few natural resources and with no established trade routes. Legally the land around Darien did not even belong to the Scots – it was Spanish territory!

What happened to the attempts to build a colony at Darien?

On 4 July 1698 five ships carrying Scots colonists left Leith harbour. When they arrived at Darien, five months later, forty-four of the would-be colonists were dead. The survivors were tired, hungry and poorly equipped. Over the next few months diseases such as malaria, yellow fever and cholera added to the death toll.

The Scots had arrived in a tropical rainforest completely unprepared for the conditions and with almost no useful trade goods or trade connections with any other area. Follow-up expeditions were sent to Darien with no overall coordinated plan. At the same time as two support ships arrived at Darien to find no sign of the first settlers, another expedition was leaving the Clyde in complete ignorance of what was happening at Darien. By the time it arrived at Darien in November 1699 over 160 people had died on the voyage.

In March 1700 the colony was abandoned. Almost 200 settlers had died. The Company of Scotland was ruined and many investors faced ruin. The Darien Scheme and the dream of a colony of New Caledonia were over.

Why did the Darien scheme fail?

The Darien Scheme was a disaster waiting to happen. Given the poor planning, underfunding and lack of experience, perhaps the colony was destined to fail. However, the colony was also a victim of European power politics and, in particular, the political ambitions of King William.

The Scottish colony at Darien was in the heart of the Spanish empire in the Americas. At that time Spain was shipping back millions of pounds worth of silver from South America. The Spanish were not prepared to let the Scots disrupt that trade. At the same time, King William had taken Britain into a war with France. William's ally against France was Spain. William did not want to annoy Spain, so he would certainly not support the Scots moving into Spanish territory. That led to William instructing English colonies in the relatively nearby West Indies to give no help at all to the stranded Scots colonists.

William and the 'Scottish problem'

Why did relations between Scotland and England seem worse than ever by 1700?

By 1700 King William was not much nearer to solving his 'Scottish problem'. Although united by a common king, Scotland felt ignored by him, because he seemed to take no interest in it. In fact, the Glencoe Massacre and the Darien Disaster came to symbolise the British monarch's alleged desire to destroy 'the Scottish threat'.

Why was William so concerned about 'the Scottish threat'?

Remember that King William was also William, Prince of Orange and military commander of the army of the Netherlands. At that time the Netherlands had ambitions to be a powerful European state and was at war with Roman Catholic France, but William's difficulties increased because of events in Spain.

The king of Spain died leaving no clear successor. The most obvious successor was a French prince, and he was invited to become king of Spain. If that happened then France and Spain could have become united as allies in a war against the Protestant states of Europe. William saw the threat of a Roman Catholic-dominated Europe and so entered a war that became known as the War of Spanish Succession (because it started as a row about who should be next in line – succeed – to the Spanish throne).

The war was really about political and economic power, not only in Europe but also in overseas colonies. Each side wanted to increase its power, and especially in overseas colonies. William not only wanted to support Holland, his home country, but also wanted to increase the power and wealth of his kingdom – and by that he thought of England, not Scotland. However, Scotland could still pose a serious threat if England's enemies somehow managed to ally with Scotland and use it as a base from which to attack England.

How did the death of William change relations between England and Scotland?

The death of King William in 1702 resulted in the succession of Queen Anne to the crowns of England and Scotland. Anne's last surviving child had died in 1700 and the English Act of Settlement of 1701 had arranged for Anne's closest Protestant relative to become Britain's next monarch. That person was Sophie and she was a princess in Hanover, Germany. The Scottish Parliament was not happy about this 'Hanoverian succession' as it was called.

The Hanoverian succession

Why did the issue of the Hanoverian succession worsen relations between England and Scotland?

From England's point of view it was unthinkable that Scotland and England should have separate monarchs, so securing the Hanoverian succession in Scotland became the English Parliament's main objective. However, the Scottish Parliament was not happy.

In earlier years the Scottish Parliament had been a 'rubber stamp' just accepting what the king or queen wanted them to accept. Now it was angry and, with its increased strength, the Scottish Parliament wanted to show that the English Parliament would not bully it over the issue of the Hanoverian succession.

What did the Scottish Parliament do to show its anger towards England?

The Scottish Parliament showed how angry it was with England by passing a series of new laws that asserted Scotland's freedom of action and also seemed very anti-English.

Approving the financial supply was vital to the running of the Scottish government and also in granting money to the Crown to allow it to pay for fighting its wars. One of the first actions of the new Scottish Parliament was to refuse to vote for a budget that would raise money to allow the government of Scotland to operate smoothly.

The Act anent (about) Peace and War stated that the Scottish Parliament's permission was needed before any king or queen of Scotland could make war, make a peace treaty or form alliances with other countries. In effect, the Scottish Parliament was saying that Scotland would make its own mind up over whether or not to support England in future wars 'and that no declaration of war without consent, shall be binding on the subjects of the Scottish Kingdom'.

King William, and then Queen Anne, knew that not only were Scottish soldiers needed to fight their wars in Europe but so was Scottish money. If Scotland did not support England's wars it would be very difficult for England to win the War of the Spanish Succession.

The Wool Act and **the Wine Act** (see below) seemed designed to boost Scottish trade at the expense of English interests. The wool trade was vital to Scotland's economy. Apart from linen, wool was **the** fibre for making almost all cloth at this time. The Wool Act encouraged Scottish exports but banned **any** wool imports from England. In economic terms such actions are called protectionist, because they protect the home industries. The Wool Act protected the Scottish wool trade but also hit the English wool trade hard. Historian Tom Devine writes, 'The Wool Act was regarded as openly hostile by England in allowing the export and prohibiting the import of wool. As such, it was viewed as an openly aggressive act against English trade.'

Was the Wine Act really anti-English?

The Wine Act of 1703 allowed foreign wines, including French wines, to be imported into Scotland. England could easily have stopped the trade between Scotland and France but trade in wines was a major part of Scotland's economy and, if the war with France (thought of in Scotland as 'England's war') caused the Scots difficulties, then ill-feeling against England would grow and grow.

Senior English politicians were growing worried that Scotland was not just angry but could become an enemy of England. Queen Anne's chief minister (rather like our prime minister today) was called Lord Godolphin, and he wanted Scottish tempers calmed down. Godolphin was well aware that wars cost money, and England needed to raise money for its wars by taxing the population. That taxation could only happen in Scotland if the Scottish Parliament approved it. By allowing the Scottish parliament to pass the Wine Act, Godolphin hoped that Scotland might be brought back on friendlier terms with England once it had passed through its 'anti-English' temper. A calmer Scotland could then be persuaded to approve the taxes needed for raising of money for the war.

Members of the Court Party in the Scottish Parliament proposed the Wine Act. The Court Party existed really just to promote the interests of the Crown and to put forward the wishes of the monarch. Scottish politicians could pretend and claim that the Wine Act had slapped England in the face but in reality the English Parliament, and Godolphin in particular, were happy to allow it to happen.

Godolphin also wanted something else from Scotland in return, and that something was linked to the **Act of Security**.

The Act of Security was passed by the Scottish Parliament in 1704 in open defiance of the Court Party and the king's ministers in Scotland. The Scottish Parliament was being deliberately provocative and in effect the Scots were offering a deal with England to allow the Hanoverian succession to go ahead.

Why did the Act of Security cause such a headache to England?

If the English did not agree to the Scots' terms, then the Scots claimed the right to choose their own successor to Queen Anne, who had to be of the royal line of Scotland and of the true Protestant religion.

The Scottish Parliament also stated that it would not accept the Hanoverian succession unless guarantees of Scottish independence from English interference were given. As an extra condition of acceptance, the Scots also wanted trading access with all of England's American colonies!

From England's point of view, the Act of Security created a major strategic and military headache. The Scots would be able to decide on their own foreign policy at a time when England was involved in the War of the Spanish Succession. The Act of Security also opened up the possibility of the Scots choosing to replace Queen Anne with a Scottish king, who might encourage a French-Scottish alliance. Such an alliance could in turn result in attacks on England from Scotland, France and even Ireland simultaneously. Godolphin knew that the Scottish 'problem' had to be neutralised and the Hanoverian succession secured. The best way to do that would be to move towards a union between England and Scotland.

Issue 2 – Arguments for and against union with England

Issue 2 is about arguments for and against union with England.

To cover the syllabus you should know about the following:

- How religious issues and the economy led to strong arguments for and against union.
- Why Scottish access to the English colonies was an important issue.
- Why Scottish identity was an issue in the arguments about union.
- How opinions about union differed in Scotland.

England was blamed for many of the difficulties faced by Scotland since 1690. The seven ill years of the 1690s had made many Scots look for reasons, explanations or excuses for their poverty. For many Scots the reasons seemed to come from England.

- Many blamed England for the failure of the Darien Scheme.
- The scandal of the Glencoe Massacre had also discredited English authority.
- By 1697, when William finally made peace with France, England's wars were seriously damaging Scottish businesses and trade. Meanwhile the Royal Navy was strictly enforcing the Navigation Acts and denying Scots trade with England's rich colonies.
- At the same time as the trade slump hit, Scottish nobles were losing money because of falling rent incomes as a result of successive bad harvests.
- To Scots all their miseries seemed rooted in the Union of the Crowns in 1603 that in some ways bound Scotland and England together.

Increasing tensions between Scotland and England

How important was the *Worcester* Incident?

The events surrounding the *Worcester* Incident showed how easily anti-English feeling could explode into violence and possibly threaten political stability in Britain.

The *Worcester* was an English ship seized in the Firth of Forth on suspicion that it was a pirate ship responsible for attacking Scottish shipping. The accusation was nonsense but the Edinburgh mob believed every rumour and story about the 'wicked pirates'. In March 1705 the captain and crew were found guilty and imprisoned in Edinburgh's tolbooth prison. On 11 April the captain of the *Worcester* and two of the crew were taken to Leith Sands and hanged for piracy in front of a mob of 80 000.

The *Worcester* Incident showed how the tensions between England and Scotland could erupt very quickly into violence. Government ministers in both countries were concerned about the damage if such tensions erupted into war. Perhaps the only way to avoid such dangers would be a union of the two countries?

Why was the English government afraid of Scotland?

The actions of the Scottish Parliament from 1703 convinced Queen Anne and her ministers that Scotland had to be brought under control. The Act of Security added to English fears. The War of Spanish Succession had started up again in 1702 and the French King Louis XIV was actively encouraging the Jacobites. At the heart of England's fears was the possibility of England's enemies using Scotland as a base for invasion. If the Scots chose their own king – possibly even a Roman Catholic Stuart – then England would be trapped between enemies to north and south.

From England's point of view Scotland was a potential threat to its security.

Queen Anne

How did England try to push Scotland towards union?

To achieve union the English Parliament decided to put more pressure on Scotland. The pressure was called the Alien Act.

The Alien Act specified that, unless they agreed to the Hanoverian succession **and** agreed to start to plan for a full union with England by Christmas Day 1705, then all Scots would be treated as foreign aliens in England.

Would the Alien Act hurt Scotland?

Yes. All trade from Scotland into England would be stopped. English goods needed and wanted in Scotland would not be available. Scottish traders could not do business with England.

Tension between the two countries increased further. There were rumours of Jacobite risings and of war between Scotland and England. English troops were sent to protect the border and Newcastle had new defences built to protect it from a possible Scottish invasion.

At this point Queen Anne used the Alien Act to pressurise the Scots. The queen ordered her ministers in Scotland to make clear that the Alien Act would be strictly enforced **unless** the Scottish Parliament accepted the Hanoverian succession or at least agreed to a union with England.

What was the Alien Act **really** meant to do?

Daniel Defoe had been sent to Scotland to work as a spy for England. His task was to report back to his English masters about how the Scots felt about union. He wrote that the Alien Act tended to make enemies of the Scottish nation and that in his opinion, the Alien Act was the most unjust act passed by the English Parliament. In his opinion, the Alien Act was far more likely to push England and Scotland apart than to pull them closer together.

However, from the English point of view, the Alien Act was never really meant to operate against Scotland. It was meant to persuade Scotland that union would be in their interest. The Alien Act showed that the usual English opposition to union had been abandoned and now England wanted to either force or persuade Scotland to accept union.

Scottish views on union

How did most Scots feel about the possibility of union?

In early 1706 a combination of Scottish and English politicians, called Commissioners, met to discuss proposals for a union between Scotland and England. The draft Treaty of Union that emerged contained twenty-five articles or parts.

As news of the contents of the draft treaty leaked out many groups in Scotland were angry, worried or fearful for the future.

Opposition to the Union came from many sections of Scottish society.

Why did the Kirk oppose union at first?

The most sustained and strongest opposition came from the Kirk, the Scottish Protestant Presbyterian Church. The Kirk feared for its independence in self-governing and in the way it worshipped. The English (Anglican) Church had different procedures and ways of worshipping. It also made use of bishops, something detested by the Kirk. Every week in churches across Scotland Scottish Presbyterian ministers preached against the union and so must have influenced a considerable amount of public opinion.

Other religious groups also opposed union, mainly because they felt that it would frustrate their own hopes and beliefs.

Roman Catholics and Episcopalians both supported the Jacobites. Jacobites wanted the return of the son of James VII as king and were totally against the Hanoverian succession. Not surprisingly, they were also totally against the union.

How did Scottish politicians feel about union?

The Court Party in the Scottish Parliament always supported union. They saw that the greatest benefit to them lay in supporting closer links with England.

In contrast, the Country Party members feared union and the loss of a Scottish Parliament. They pointed out that any Parliament based in London would automatically swamp Scottish interests just because there were far more English members than Scottish. Andrew Fletcher of Saltoun, near Haddington, was a Commissioner in the old Parliament of Scotland. He argued against full union with England. Fletcher did not believe that the separate interests of England and Scotland could be served in one united Parliament. He declared that the Scots would deserve no pity if they voluntarily surrendered their separate interests to the mercy of a united Parliament, where the English had so vast a majority.

Lord Belhaven was also against a full incorporating union. He believed that in England nothing would change. There would be the same Parliament and the same taxes whereas Scotland would lose its Parliament, its laws, its taxation system and much of its separate identity. He finished his speech in Parliament by asking, 'Good God. Is this an entire surrender?'

Were there strong economic arguments for union?

Some Scots wondered if union would help Scotland become more prosperous. It can be argued that the Darien Disaster had ironically increased moves towards a union between Scotland and England. From the Scots' point of view there seemed no way out of the economic mess of post-Darien Scotland. Perhaps union with England would be the only way of getting some money back into Scotland?

From an English point of view union with Scotland would stop a Scottish Parliament encouraging competition with English trading interests simply because a Scottish Parliament would no longer exist!

Is there any evidence of public opinion in Scotland just before the union?

Most public opinion seems to have been be very much against union. Anti-union riots broke out in Glasgow, Stirling, Dumfries and Edinburgh. However, it is difficult to judge how much the riots represented public opinion, as the actions of the mobs could be whipped up easily by stories and rumours.

Daniel Defoe, the English spy, reported back to London on how the Scots felt about union. He described how he found the whole of Edinburgh in uproar and how mobs of people marched up and down the High Street beating drums and shouting 'No Union' and 'Death to the English'. More educated members of the public, especially business people, were concerned about the effects of union on Scotland. They feared that Scotland would have to pay very high taxes and obey English laws because there would not be sufficient Scottish MPs in the new British Parliament to protect Scottish interests.

The number of petitions received for and against union might be a more accurate way of showing public opinion. The Scottish Parliament received ninety-one petitions from across Scotland showing worries about taxation, competition from English trade, loss of sovereignty and fears about religious freedom.

However, pro-unionist politicians such as the Duke of Argyll rejected these petitions and called them 'paper kites'. Argyll did not believe that the petitions represented opinion across Scotland. On the other hand, there was **not one** petition supporting union.

Why did union happen when so much of Scotland was against it?

The short answer is that the bulk of the population had no say in political decision-making. Union came about mainly because England wanted it and a group of Scottish politicians saw it as in their interests to ensure it happened.

As rumours of war between England and Scotland spread in 1706 and early 1707 politicians on both sides of the border decided it was time to cool things down.

When a new Scottish Parliament met in June 1705, only one month after the Alien Act became law, it was clear that most Scottish opinion was against union. Many Scots were still very angry with the Alien Act. However, some Scots politicians began to read the Alien Act more closely. They realised that the Alien Act was the English reaction to all the acts passed by the Scottish Parliament that had provoked England. They also noted that the Alien Act argued that a union would be the best way to maintain peace between the two countries. The Act stated that its intention was 'to prevent the many inconveniences which may speedily happen to the two kingdoms of England and Scotland [such as war] if a more complete union be not made between the said Kingdoms.'

Nevertheless, as far as many Scots were concerned, the Alien Act was a barrier to union. The Scottish Parliament would not even consider a union unless the threat of the Alien Act was removed. Consequently the Scottish Parliament wrote to Queen Anne saying they were interested in forming a union but **not** as long as the Alien Act stayed in operation. Very soon afterwards the English Parliament scrapped the Alien Act. The way was now clear for discussions to start about a union.

Issue 3 – The passing of the Act of Union

Issue 3 is about the passing of the Act of Union.

To cover the syllabus you should know about the following:

- Why England became more positive towards the idea of union.
- What the difference is between a federal and an incorporating union.
- What the role of the Commissioners was.
- How the Act of Union was finally passed.

England and the benefits of union

Why did Queen Anne and the English Parliament want union?

There is no doubt that England moved towards union for the benefit of England.

From an English viewpoint union with Scotland would help England's military, trading and political interests. Scots could serve in the British army and fight in England's wars. Scottish business and trading skills would help in the growth and development of England's colonies and its industries. As an extra bonus Scotland, like England, would remain a Protestant country. Daniel Defoe wrote that the benefits of a union with Scotland would be peace, an increase in the strength of England and it would 'shut the back door' to the danger of invasion from the north and possible war with Scotland. Another writer, Dean Swift, said at the time that union with Scotland was wanted not for any direct good it could do England but that union would help to avoid a probable evil.

Perhaps it was not so much a case of England wanting union but rather that England **needed** a union with Scotland – and the type of union that England wanted was all or nothing, i.e. a full incorporating union.

What is the difference between a federal union and an incorporating union?

A federal union would mean that some form of Scottish self-government would still exist but also that Scottish representatives would be sent to the united Parliament in England. A federal union would be similar to what exists today, with a Scottish Parliament dealing with things Scottish and the London-based Parliament dealing with British issues. We have MSPs and also MPs. Many Scots supported this compromise union. A full incorporating union meant there would be only one Parliament in London. The Scots would send some representatives to it.

With only one Parliament ruling Britain and with English representatives always in a majority this would be the best way to ensure Scotland's loyalty and the Hanoverian succession. England wanted all or nothing. Throughout the discussions England only ever wanted an incorporating union.

Godolphin and the queen's ministers believed that a full incorporating union could be the answer to all England's worries. With a full incorporating union there would be no separate Scottish Parliament and therefore no 'Scottish problems'. Decisions taken by the bigger British Parliament would be put into action in Scotland as well as England. So Scotland would get the Hanoverian succession whether they liked it or not. It was win/win for England. The other type of union – the federal union – was never a serious option for England.

Scotland divided

How divided was the Scottish Parliament on the eve of union?

Opinion in Scotland was divided over the question of union, with most people certainly against an incorporating union. The Scottish Parliament was likewise divided.

There were four main groups in Parliament.

The Court Party, predictably, supported union. The Court Party was made up of politicians appointed by the queen, and existed almost entirely to represent the wishes of the English Parliament in Scotland. Although many of Scotland's nobility linked themselves to the Court Party in Parliament, it was not a political party in the modern sense. The Court Party was simply a collection of nobles who saw an advantage in being seen as supporters of the queen. The advantage would mean promotion, well-paid jobs and pensions. Large landowners and noblemen such as the Duke of Hamilton and the Duke of Queensberry profited personally and politically from their association with the Court Party.

Duke of Hamilton

Duke of Queensberry

However, if the nobles ceased to see an advantage in supporting the queen, they would look for personal advantage elsewhere.

The Country Party was against union. Their most famous members were the Earl of Belhaven and Fletcher of Saltoun.

Earl of Belhaven

Fletcher of Saltoun

The New Party became known as the Squadrone Volante, which means 'the Flying Squadron'. They got that nickname because they kept flying from side to side in the debates about union. The Squadrone Volante was a group of about thirty Scottish MPs whose members were moderate Presbyterians who opposed the Episcopalians and the Jacobites. Not surprisingly, the Squadrone Volante supported the Hanoverian succession because it would stop the return of the Roman Catholic Stuarts. The Squadrone Volante was less consistent in its attitudes towards union. At first the Squadrone Volante was against a union but during the debates over union in 1706–07 it changed its policy and supported full union with England. When the Squadrone Volante joined with the Court Party to support union it was inevitable that union would happen.

The final group in the Scottish Parliament was made up of **Jacobites.** They were never really a political party but because they supported the return of a Stuart and Roman Catholic king against the wishes of Parliament they were called the Cavalier party. The Cavaliers had fought against Parliament in the Civil War fifty years before.

What was the role of the Commissioners in moving Scotland towards union?

Arguments about the proposed union went on day after day in the Scottish Parliament. In an attempt to break the deadlock it was agreed that two groups of Commissioners, one from Scotland and one from England, should negotiate a union. Given the mood of Parliament and public opinion across Scotland it was clear the Scottish Commissioners would oppose union. Then the Duke of Hamilton made a surprise move. Hamilton was a leading figure in the Country Party and a leader of opposition to the union.

To everyone's surprise, Hamilton suddenly suggested that the choice of Scottish Commissioners should be left to the queen. Naturally, the Court Party was delighted. The queen would of course choose as commissioners Scottish MPs who were mostly for the union. Not all Commissioners were supporters of union. In fact, one was a Jacobite. However, the few who were against union were easily outnumbered and outvoted, by the majority of Commissioners in favour of union.

Scotland and England had thirty-one Commissioners each. They began work in April 1707 and within ten days they had agreed the outline arrangements for a union. Within ten weeks the details of union had been agreed.

How important were the actions of the Duke of Hamilton to passing the Treaty of Union?

Hamilton's change of policy made union inevitable. Hamilton kept letting his followers down. When there was a possibility of an armed uprising against the union in the south-west of Scotland, Hamilton called off the action. When a boycott in the Scottish Parliament to hold up discussion of the union was threatened, Hamilton stopped that too.

Hamilton's actions led to a suspicion that he had been bribed. Historians have pointed out that Hamilton was heavily in debt and was facing the possibility of losing recently gained estates in England if union failed. Suspicions about Hamilton's real interests were raised further when, after the Treaty of Union was passed, Hamilton was rewarded with titles and money.

There is no proof that Hamilton was bribed to change his mind and support the union, but four years later, he was given land in England when he became the Duke of Brandon. Was that his reward for his help in passing the treaty? The strong suspicion lingers on!

Why did the Treaty of Union pass through the Scottish Parliament so quickly?

Parliament ignored popular opposition to union. Strong feelings on the issues of national identity and loss of sovereignty (political independence) were not enough to stop the Treaty of Union being passed in the Scottish Parliament.

Political opposition to the Treaty of Union was divided and ineffective. Members of the Country Party could not cooperate with the Cavalier Party, as they disagreed over the return of a Stuart king.

One of the most decisive reasons for the Treaty of Union passing through the Scottish Parliament fairly quickly was because its supporters stayed united. The pro-union Court Party knew it was in their own interests to support union.

Scottish politicians who supported union and voted for it in the Scottish Parliament were often rewarded with titles and money. This is called self-interest. For example, the Earl of Roxburghe was a member of the Squadrone Volante. He had been against union but after he and his party changed their minds and supported union he was rewarded with land and the title of Duke of Roxburghe.

What immediate advantages would Scotland gain from union?

In October 1706 the Scottish Parliament began discussing the twenty-five draft Articles of Union.

At first the negotiations over union went nowhere fast.

Discussions then sped up when the Scots realised there were several advantages for them in a union with England.

- Scotland would be allowed to trade with England's colonies. Trading rights with England's colonies would help Scotland recover from the disasters of the 1690s.
- The Scottish Presbyterian Kirk was given guarantees that it would be free from English influence. On 12 November 1706 an Act for Securing the Protestant Religion and Presbyterian Church Government became law. Almost immediately the Kirk dropped its opposition to union and then took little further part in the discussions.
- The Alien Act would be scrapped and would not be used against Scotland.
- Scotland would be protected from any attempts by Roman Catholic France to help the Jacobites start a war in Scotland against England.
- Scots feared the powerful English armies. If the Scots rejected union perhaps England would invade Scotland and force union on Scotland? English troops were gathered in the north of England and in Northern Ireland for a swift move into Scotland if the Treaty of Union was rejected. The threat from England was obvious. Many Scots would rather voluntarily accept a negotiated union than have one forced upon them.

- The Scots gained compensation for the Darien Disaster. Although the terms of union insisted that the Company of Scotland was forced to end all its business and was wound up, people who had invested in the Darien Scheme and then lost money were compensated and even got a small dividend (profit) back on their investment.

What were the main terms of the Treaty of Union?

The new Kingdom of Great Britain began on 1 May 1707.
The Scots had tried to negotiate a federal union but the English Commissioners would not accept that. England wanted, and got, a full incorporating union.

A new flag was created out of a combination of the crosses of St George and St Andrew.

Scotland kept its own legal system.

Future kings and queens all had to be Protestant. Both countries accepted the Hanoverian succession.

The Scottish Parliament was abolished.
There was to be only one Parliament. In reality, the English Parliament continued as it always had been and the Scots fitted in to the English system.

Scots were to have forty-five MPs in the House of Commons and sixteen Lords in the House of Lords. Originally England had wanted to base Scottish representation on the share of national taxation paid by Scotland. That would have given the Scots far fewer representatives. The Scots argued that representation in the Westminster Parliament should be based on the size of the Scottish population compared to that of England. That would have given the Scots far more MPs and Lords. In the end a compromise was reached.

Scotland and England were joined economically.
Economically, the new Great Britain was to have one currency, with the same system of weights and measures. Scottish ships and merchants had open access to all English ports in Britain and the colonies.

Scotland had to share England's national debt.
Before union, Scotland had almost no national debt. The national debt is the amount of money that the government of a country has borrowed from banks or other financial institutions to pay for expenses such as wars. When Scotland became part of Great Britain, it had to take on a share of England's national debt – and that was huge! Governments raise money by raising taxes, so the national debt of any country really has to be paid back from the taxes paid by the people of the country. In 1707 England had a huge national debt, partly because of all the wars it was involved in. The Scots now had to pay their share of the debt.

Naturally, the Scots complained about paying towards England's national debt. They argued it was not their debt and Scotland was a poor country. The result was that Scotland was paid compensation to help ease the tax burden. The compensation was called the **Equivalent**.

The Equivalent totalled nearly £400 000, about £26 million pounds in today's money. That money included all unpaid back pay, which the Crown in Scotland owed its officials.

Scotland gained tax breaks to allow it to adjust economically to union with England.
For the first seven years after union Scotland would not pay the taxes on salt and on malt used for brewing. Other tax breaks added to the feeling that Scotland was being given financial incentives to accept the Union. For example, Scotland's wool industry received £2000 each year for seven years and then the same amount was to be used to help other industries in Scotland.

Despite strong arguments and emotional speeches against union, the Great Nobles of Scotland voted overwhelmingly for the Treaty of Union. Although the majority of Country and Burgh Commissioners also voted for the union, the difference between those for and those against was not so clear-cut.

In January 1707 the Scottish Parliament passed all twenty-five Articles of Union and in March 1707 the English Parliament also agreed to the union. On 25 March 1707, the Scottish Parliament met for the last time until 1999.

The Duke of Queensberry announced 'the public business of this session being now over, it is full time to put an end to it'.

How true is it that Scotland was bought and sold by English gold?

When Sir John Clerk of Penicuik stated that the Treaty of Union had been signed against the wishes of three-quarters of Scotland's population no one disputed the figure. The realisation that most Scots were totally against the incorporating union established in 1707 led some to suspect that members of the Scottish Parliament were 'persuaded' to support union by promises of rewards of some sort. For example, although it was claimed that the Equivalent was paid to compensate Scotland for inheriting a proportion of England's high tax bill, a lot of the money was used to compensate investors who had lost money in the Darien Scheme. It just so happened that many of those same investors were members of the Squadrone Volante, the group that changed sides in the union debate and in so doing made the passing of the Act of Union so much easier! Just months before the union debate, the Squadrone Volante had been strongly anti-union. Suddenly, in the union debate in Parliament all twenty-five members of the group voted for the union!

Eighty years after the union Robert Burns wrote his poem 'Such a Parcel o' Rogues in a Nation' as a protest about the Act of Union.

> Fareweel to a' our Scottish fame,
> Fareweel our ancient glory;
> Fareweel ev'n to the Scottish name,
> Sae fam'd in martial story.
>
> What force or guile could not subdue,
> Thro' many warlike ages,
> Is wrought now by a coward few,
> For hireling traitor's wages.
>
> But English gold has been our bane -
> Such a parcel o' rogues in a nation!

The 'parcel o' rogues' refers to the Scottish politicians who, Burns believed, had betrayed Scotland for 'English gold'. The feeling that Scotland was sold out by politicians bribed by England lingers on.

In August 1706, two months before the Scottish Parliament was due to consider the twenty-five Articles of Union the Duke of Queensberry asked for and received from Lord Godolphin a sum of £20 000 – more than £2·5 million in today's money. Critics of the union say that Queensberry was building up a fund of money that he would use to bribe other Scottish politicians.

The support of the Court Party was vital, and members of the party had to be politically managed to ensure their continued support. When we examine the evidence that the Duke of Argyll was given a military promotion, became a lord and was given money with a value today of £1·3 million, it is difficult not to suspect some bribery at work.

The earliest claims of bribery came from George Lockhart, who stated that the English treasury had secretly given money to thirty-two members of the Scottish Parliament. However, recent research has shown that most of the money was used to pay overdue wages and salaries owing to government ministers and officials, including several Scottish nobles. It is also true that Lockhart was a Jacobite and so had his own reasons for spreading rumours about the honesty of politicians who accepted the Hanoverian settlement.

The largest amount, £12 325, was paid to Queensberry himself but, as the queen's Lord High Commissioner, Queensberry was already a supporter of union so what was the point of bribing him? What is clear is that Queensberry claimed salary arrears of over £26 000, yet was paid less than half that amount.

A more realistic reply to the claims of bribery is that most Scottish politicians accepted that a union of some kind was a necessary solution to Scotland's economic problems. With so many politicians accepting the need for union there was simply no need for widespread bribery. In truth, it appears that payouts from the fund of £20 000 may have directly influenced the votes of no more than four or five members of the Scottish Parliament.

Issue 4 – The effects of the union, to 1740

Issue 4 is about the effects of the union up to 1740.

To cover the syllabus you should be aware of the following:

- How the union affected Scottish agriculture, manufacturing and trade.
- What the political effects of the union were.
- How the union affected the Hanoverian succession.
- Why a Jacobite rising happened in 1715.

Discontent in Scotland

Why were Scots unhappy with union only a few years after it happened?

In the years immediately after union many Scots felt it was not bringing the benefits they thought it would deliver. There was even a feeling that England was breaking its promises.

The Kirk had opposed the union until England made promises to protect the Scottish Presbyterian religion. Within five years of the union three new laws were passed that made it look as if the Scottish Presbyterian Kirk was under threat.

First of all, the Toleration Act of 1712 allowed Scottish Episcopalians the right to worship freely and without persecution from Presbyterians. Presbyterians thought this was just the start of building up Episcopalianism in Scotland and then bringing an Anglican style of church worship back into Scotland.

Secondly, the Patronage Act of 1712 gave the right to choose Church ministers to the local landowners. One of the core beliefs of Presbyterianism is that the members of the congregation – the members of the Kirk, who worship in the local church – should make the choice of minister, but many landowners were Episcopalian. The Kirk was unhappy about Episcopalians choosing its ministers. The Kirk members were also worried that the Patronage Act, along with the Toleration Act, might even lead to bishops being brought back in to manage the Kirk.

Finally, the Yule Vacance Act ordered that Christmas Day should be a holiday, at least in the Scottish law courts! Presbyterians were angry. They believed that midwinter holidays such as Christmas were the remnants of old pagan celebrations and Roman Catholic habits.

From an English point of view the three Acts seemed reasonable. From Presbyterian Scotland's point of view the three Acts were part of a deliberate attempt to destroy Presbyterian beliefs and broke promises made by England during the debates over union.

How were Scots angered by new taxation?

After the war against the French ended in 1713, England started to raise taxation on Scottish trade. New taxes on salt, beer, linen, soap and malt forced up prices. Salt, for example, was a vital product used to preserve food. The new taxes doubled the price. Malt is a vital ingredient in ale and beer making. The terms of union had stated that a tax on malt would not be changed, but when a malt tax was proposed in 1713 riots erupted across Scotland. Although the tax was postponed until 1725, the resentment towards union continued.

Relations between England and Scotland were made worse by smuggling. From England's point of view, Scotland was cheating. The union had allowed Scots to trade with English colonies and Glasgow was growing rich on the tobacco trade. However, much of the tobacco coming from America was smuggled into Scotland with no taxation paid. The London-based treasury was losing huge amounts of money to smuggling.

Scotland argued it was only being taxed to pay for England's wars and so up and down Scotland small wars were fought between smugglers and the customs officers sent to stop the smuggling. Smugglers became local heroes and customs officers were seen as hated officials trying to enforce unfair taxes.

People in England felt Scotland was being unreasonable and argued that the union was never intended to be an equal partnership. In some ways England believed it had 'bought' Scotland and could do as it wished.

How did English law seem to be of greater importance than Scots law?

The union had promised that Scottish law would be respected, but in 1709 the English Treason Act was extended to Scotland. This broke a promise in the Act of Union but England argued it made Scotland and England more secure against any Jacobite threat.

Another threat to Scottish law came in 1708, just one year after union. In Scotland the Court of Session was the most important law court in the country. Once a decision had been made there it could not be challenged in Scotland. However, after union, people unhappy with Court of Session decisions took their complaint to the House of Lords in London. That was against the rules of the union and it implied that Scotland and England were not equal partners.

Why were Scottish nobles and big landowners unhappy about political changes after union?

Before the union one of the most important parts of the Scottish government was the Privy Council. The Privy Council contained ministers trusted by the king or queen and was a vital part of managing Scotland. To many Scots nobles, membership of the Privy Council was a guaranteed path to promotion, money and top jobs for themselves and their relatives. Suddenly, only two months after the union, the Privy Council was abolished by the London-based Parliament. Of course, many Scots MPs also voted to abolish the Privy Council because they felt it operated as a private club for the Scottish nobility only and deserved to be swept away.

Also, Scottish nobles who had been made lords were refused entry to the House of Lords in London. It seemed that Scots who were made into lords under a British Parliament were not as important as English lords!

Was there really serious discontent with the union in the years immediately after 1707?

Yes, there was, even to the extent that in 1713 Scotland was ready to break the union. The Kirk felt threatened by what it saw as the broken promises of the union. Many Scots were angry about high levels of taxation on products that they considered daily necessities. East coast ports and harbours were declining because of a loss of trade due to 'England's wars' in Europe. Scottish nobles and their families saw their hopes of gaining power and making money from the union fading fast.

In 1713 a proposal was made in the London Parliament that the union should be ended. Even many English MPs agreed. The vote was very close, with the proposal only being defeated by four votes. Just a few years after the union was agreed, it was by no means certain that it would last. Such a situation pleased the Jacobites. They hoped to gain support from discontented Scots.

Did the Jacobites really threaten the union with England?

The Jacobites were against the union. By the terms of the union treaty the Scots accepted the Hanoverian succession. That meant the Roman Catholic Stuarts had no chance of regaining the throne of Scotland peacefully. Since so many Scots seemed to be unhappy with the union, the Jacobites thought they might have a chance to grab power in Scotland if they got help from France, who was England's enemy. France saw an opportunity to invade Scotland under the pretext of helping the Jacobites.

Why did the Jacobite rising of 1708 fail?

King Louis XIV of France believed the promises made by Scottish Jacobites that Scots were so angry about the Union that the whole of Scotland would rise up to support the return of James Stuart as their king.

King Louis hoped that a Jacobite rising in Scotland would force British armies to be diverted away from mainland Europe, where France was at war with Britain. In March 1708 a French fleet of twenty ships sailed for Scotland to help the Jacobites – then everything went wrong. The French fleet met bad weather and was then chased by the English fleet. James Stuart became ill and the French commanders lacked clear organisation and enthusiasm for their task. When the French finally reached Scotland they found little support for a Jacobite rising. Faced with inevitable failure, the French cut their losses and returned to France leaving the Jacobite rising of 1708 to fade into memory.

The 1715 Jacobite uprising

Why was there a Jacobite uprising in 1715?

By 1715 there was even more discontent with the union in Scotland. The Jacobites were ready to try again. Queen Anne had died in 1714 and the Hanoverian succession had come into operation. Next in line to the throne was a little-known German prince called George, who spoke almost no English and relied on one political group to help him. That group was called the Whig party. The opposition party was called Tory and they knew they would get no favours from the new King George. Some Tories began to plot with the Jacobites to get rid of George.

Jacobites felt the terms of the union had been broken by England. New laws such as the Patronage Act and the Toleration Act plus new taxation laws made some Jacobites think that England had no intention of keeping to the terms of the union.

Many Jacobites were Roman Catholic or Episcopalian and wanted to weaken the power of the Presbyterian Kirk in Scotland. They also knew they could not expect promotions or good jobs or pensions from the new London-based government, so Jacobite clan chiefs knew they had little to lose.

The leader of the Jacobite rising of 1715 was the Earl of Mar. He is a good example of a man who supported the Jacobites at least partly for personal interest. He had previously supported the Court Party in Scotland and also supported the union. However, when George became king, the Earl of Mar was out of favour. He could expect no promotions so he changed sides and supported the Jacobite cause. For that reason Mar became known as Bobbing John – someone who bobbed about or switched sides for his own gain.

Why did the 1715 Jacobite rising fail?

At first all went well. Most of the clansmen in northern Scotland supported the rising. The Earl of Mar raised the Jacobite flag at Braemar and, when the 'Old Pretender' James VIII landed at Peterhead, towns such as Aberdeen, Perth and Inverness declared their support for him. So why did the rising collapse?

Government forces moved rapidly to Stirling Castle and blocked the routes of the Jacobite army southwards. Mar and his Jacobite army were stopped at the battle of Sheriffmuir. He could not link up with Jacobites further south and he retreated north again.

Meanwhile in southern Scotland Presbyterian Lowland Scots feared that the return of a Stuart king would also mean the return of a Roman Catholic king. Trade was growing around Glasgow and the west of Scotland. On balance Lowland Scots decided it was in their own best interests to support 'the wee German Lairdie' as they called the new King George. The self-interest of Lowland Scots doomed the Jacobite cause.

Peace, stability and the union secure

What did the government do to make the union more secure by the 1740s?

By the 1740s Scotland was much more settled. The earlier irritations and anger about the union had faded. Better relations between England and Scotland were not accidental. English policy towards Scotland became focused on making Scotland happier with the union.

The government was careful to undermine support for the Jacobite cause. There was a very deliberate attempt to avoid revenge actions against Jacobites after 1715. The government did not want to create more enemies for itself.

In Scotland there was only one execution of a Jacobite rebel after the 1715 rising, while in England there were forty such executions. Scottish lawyers prevented most estates belonging to Jacobites from being confiscated, and most Jacobite prisoners faced trial in Scotland, not in England. As a result Scots felt the Jacobite rebels had been fairly treated.

Loyalty was also enforced more directly in the Jacobite Highlands by a network of good quality roads, bridges and forts built by General Wade. The rapid movement of troops made it much more difficult for Jacobite rebellion to take root in the Highlands.

The result of the government policy was that support for Jacobites fell rapidly. The union was secure.

How did the political management of Scotland improve?

The Whig politicians in Parliament played a smart game. They knew that Scotland was unhappy, so they began to treat Scotland carefully. The important nobles of Scotland and the ministers of the Kirk were kept happy.

The Earl of Islay, later Duke of Argyll, became the unofficial 'King of Scotland'. His job was to create political stability in Scotland and organise the support of most Scottish MPs for government policy. In return Islay was given control over a huge system of patronage, promotions and pensions to use as political 'glue' to ensure loyalty to the new government of Great Britain.

By the 1740s it was clear that Scotland was being governed in much the same way as it had been before the union.

Why had the Scottish economy improved by the 1740s?

Scotland benefited from English support to improve its farming, industry and transport. As early as 1723 the Society of Improvers in the Knowledge of Agriculture in Scotland was formed to help improve farming methods, with its main aim being to find ways to make the Highlands more economically productive. Other organisations were set up to teach and encourage new methods of production in linen and wool. Fishing was also helped and new ideas to improve production were spread through the Board of Trustees for Manufactures and Fisheries.

Exports of cattle to England increased, but the real boom in the economy happened around Glasgow. Scotland profited hugely from trade with English colonies in America and the West Indies, importing large amounts of tobacco and sugar. In exchange the west coast ports exported finished manufactured products to the colonists such as soap, cloth and guns.

England and England's colonies also provided opportunities for Scots to migrate and prosper around the world. By 1740, for the majority of Scots, concern over issues about religion and politics had faded to be replaced by the opportunities for prosperity offered by trade and industry as part of Great Britain.

Once Scots saw the advantages that the union brought in terms of peace, stability and increasing prosperity, there was simply no interest in upsetting a system that benefited most of them.

The Treaty of Union, 1689–1740: a perspective

This final section will not be part of your exam. There will be no questions linked to it. However, you should be able to reflect on the union and its effects on the development of Scottish identity.

The end of old Scotland?

The battle of Culloden in April 1746 was the last battle to be fought on British soil. In many ways it represented the end of an old, out-dated Scotland and the start of a new Scotland. The battle marked the end of issues raised throughout this study of the Treaty of Union.

The battle of Culloden marked the end of the Jacobite cause and secured completely the Hanoverian succession. Culloden was not a battle between Scotland and England. There were more Scots at Culloden fighting against Bonnie Prince Charlie than were fighting for him. The battle of Culloden marked the beginning of a new Scotland that saw its future as being part of the Union.

Did the union leave its mark on Scotland today?

In the century that followed the union, Scotland underwent industrial and agricultural revolutions that changed its urban and rural landscapes.

Trade with the American colonies transformed Glasgow. The age of the 'Tobacco Lords' left its marks on the architecture and street names of 'the second city of the Empire'.

Edinburgh became the artistic centre of Europe – the 'Athens of the North'. Even today the layout of Edinburgh's New Town reflects Scotland's confidence within the union. James Craig's plan for the New Town celebrated the union of the two nations. An understanding of the issue of the Hanoverian succession explains why Hanover Street, George Street, Frederick Street and Princes Street are so named! St Andrew Square was originally balanced by St George Square (renamed Charlotte Square) while the minor Rose and Thistle Streets are obviously named after the national emblems.

How did the union change Scotland's place in the world?

In the years following the union, Scots made their mark around the world and the area that was once the British Empire became filled with Scottish names.

For 200 years after the union Scots thought of themselves as British and were happy to be part of Britain and its empire. Being part of Britain offered Scots many opportunities. Scotland was part of the world's leading industrial and military superpower – Great Britain. Scots shared in the nationalist pride of the British Empire where they saw themselves as equal partners with the English as statesmen, engineers, businessmen and soldiers.

Scottish soldiers were seen as brave, loyal and trustworthy, men who could be relied on to fight to the end for their friends, their regiment and their country – Britain. Between 1777 and 1800 the Highlands produced more than twenty regiments for the British army. Highland soldiers were given new chiefs within the army, wore the kilt which was officially adopted as part of their uniform and marched to the sound of bagpipes wherever they were sent to expand the British Empire.

In the 19th century the stories of Sir Walter Scott added to the romantic image of Scotland that reached its peak with Queen Victoria's royal approval of all things tartan and 'Highland'. The royal family still keep alive this connection to the Highlands with their 'holiday home' at Balmoral.

Even the less romantic reality of the Highland Clearances had links with the union. The 'push' of evictions had some of their causes in the desire to change, modernise and make the Highlands more 'economically efficient'. At the same time the colonies within the former English empire provided a safety valve for some and a 'pull' for other Scottish emigrants.

The union – good or bad?

Before 1914 and the start of the Great War the central belt of Scotland was a powerhouse for the production of coal, iron and steel, shipbuilding and engineering. It was only when that powerhouse fell on hard times that Scots once again looked to the past and began to question the wisdom of the union. However, supporters of the union would argue that the growth in support for Scottish nationalism in the last fifty years must be balanced against the benefits of the union that Scotland experienced over the last 250 years.

Example question 1

Here is an example of a 'How useful' question linked to Issue 3 of the Treaty of Union special topic.

Source A is from the *Memoirs* of Lockhart of Carnwath, written in 1714.

> The ministers were concerned about the government of the Kirk, and roared against the wicked union from their pulpits, and sent addresses against it from several presbyteries and the Assembly. But no sooner did Parliament pass an Act for the security of the Kirk than most of their zeal was cooled, and many of them changed their tune and preached in favour of it.
>
> But the truth of the matter lies here: a sum of money was necessary to be distributed amongst the Scots. And this distribution of it amongst the proprietors of the Company of Scotland was the best way of bribing a nation ... alas it had the desired effect.

Question

How useful is source A as evidence of the methods used to pass the Treaty of Union?

In reaching a conclusion you should refer to:

- the origin and possible purpose of the source
- the content of the source
- recalled knowledge.

Writing your answer

Use the following advice to help write a fluent answer.

- *Paragraph 1*
  Write about the **origin** and **purpose** of the source. Why does the fact that it was written by Lockhart of Carnwath make it more or less useful in terms of the question? Why do you think it was written (its purpose)? Why does the purpose help to make the source useful?
- *Paragraph 2*
  Refer to **one** point from the source and explain why it helps make the source useful. Develop the point made by using your own knowledge.
- *Paragraph 3*
  Refer to another point from the source and explain why it helps make the source useful. Develop the point made by using your own knowledge.
- *Paragraph 4*
  Finally, refer to a third piece of evidence from the source and explain why it helps make the source useful. Develop the point made by using your own knowledge.
- *Paragraph 5*
  Reach a final conclusion about how useful the source is. Mention the reasons that you think **do** make it useful, then include any reasons you can think of that might limit the usefulness of the source. What you have done is reached a **balanced conclusion**.

How many marks would you give?

- Is there a direct comment on how the **origin** and **purpose** of the source help to make it useful? You can get **up to** 2 marks for doing that.
- Are there three different points taken from the source? Are the points developed (explained) and is it clear why these points help to make the source useful? You can get **up to** 2 marks for doing that.
- Is there some recall used either to develop points in the source or used in the balance section to suggest the source is not as useful as it could be? You can get **up to** 2 marks for doing that.

Example question 2

Here is an example of a comparison question, linked to Issue 2 of the Treaty of Union special topic. Remember that comparison questions can be used to assess **any** of the issues. Look back to page 6 and read what you have to do to answer a comparison-type question.

Source B is from the Earl of Seafield's letters.

> My reasons for joining with England on good terms were these: that the kingdom of England is a Protestant kingdom and that, therefore, the joining with them was a security for our religion. Secondly, England has trade and other advantages to give us, which no other kingdom could offer. Thirdly, England has freedom and liberty, and joining with them was the best way to secure that to us; and fourthly, I saw no other method for securing peace, the two kingdoms being in the same island, and foreign assistance was both dangerous to ourselves and England. Therefore, I was for the treaty.

Source C is from a petition against the proposed union sent from Stirling Town Council in November 1707.

> We desire that true peace and friendship be always cultivated with our neighbour England, upon just and honourable terms ... Yet we judge that going into this Treaty will bring a burden of taxation upon this land, which freedom of trade will never repay ... Scotland would still be under the regulations of the English in the Parliament of Britain, who may if they please discourage the most valuable branches of our trade, if we in any way are seen to interfere with their own. It will ruin our manufactories, our religion, laws and liberties. As a result, one of the most ancient nations so long and so gloriously defended will be suppressed. Our parliament and all that is dear to us will be extinguished.

Question

To what extent do sources B and C agree in their attitudes towards union?

Compare the content overall and in detail.

Writing your answer

Use the following advice to help write a fluent answer.

- *Paragraph 1*
  Start by writing your overall comparison – do sources B and C agree or disagree over how they felt about Union with England?
- *Paragraphs 2–5*
  Deal with one detailed comparison in each paragraph. Find four points of comparison that the sources agree or disagree about. Explain each comparison fully by using brief quotes from the source and your own recalled knowledge.

How many marks would you give?

- Is there an overall comparison summing up the main difference between the sources? You can give a mark for that.
- Apart from the overall comparison, are there four more direct comparisons made, and is each comparison well explained and not just a series of quotes from the sources? If the answer is yes then give 1 mark for each clear and correct comparison.

> **Top Tip**
> **Usually** in a comparison question you can gain marks for identifying and explaining points where the sources agree **and also** where they disagree. Don't always assume that the sources will take exactly opposite points of view. They might – but not always.

Example question 3

Here is an example of a 'How far...' question, linked to Issue 1 of the Treaty of Union. Remember that 'How far...' questions can be used to assess **any** of the issues. Look back to page 6 and read what you have to do to answer a 'How far...' type question.

Source D is from *1707: The Union of Scotland and England* (1979) by P. H. Scott.

> The Scottish Parliament turned to measures designed to restore Scottish trade from the effects of a century of neglect and discrimination. In 1695 it passed an Act for a company trading to Africa and the Indies. This was the Company of Scotland, which as the first of its ventures, decided to settle a colony at Darien. William, as King of Scotland, agreed to the Act and signed the Charter of the Company. As King of England, he was obliged to do all he could to sabotage and oppose the efforts of the Company.
>
> When the Darien scheme failed, it was largely due to mismanagement and inadequate preparation. Many asked how a country could succeed when its own Head of State actively opposed its interests.
>
> At this critical moment, when relations between the two countries were as bad as they had ever been, a dynastic accident offered a solution. The last child of Queen Anne died in 1700. In 1701, the English Parliament, without consultation with Scotland, passed the Act of Settlement, passing the succession after Anne to the Electress Sophia of Hanover.

Question

How far does source D show the increasing tensions between Scotland and England before the union?

Writing your answer

Use the following advice to help write a fluent answer.

The source comments on examples of increasing tensions between Scotland and England before the union such as the Darien disaster, the Hanoverian Succession, King William's attitude towards Scotland and problems faced by Scottish trade. Write a brief paragraph on each of the reasons for tension mentioned in the source.

Use your own knowledge first of all to develop and explain more fully the examples of increasing tension identified in the source. For example, you could write about the Navigation Acts and how they damaged Scottish trade or you could provide details about the Darien Disaster and how Darien's failure increased tension between Scots and English.

You should then use your own knowledge to write about other reasons for increased tension not been mentioned in the source.

How many marks would you give?

- Does your answer clearly select four different reasons for increasing tension between England and Scotland before Union and explain them briefly? You can give **up to** 4 marks for doing that.
- Does your answer provide balance by using a lot of recall about other reasons for increasing tension? You can give **up to** 7 marks for that.

Example question 4

Here is an example of a 'How fully...' question, linked to Issue 4 of the Treaty of Union. Remember that 'How fully...' questions, like all the other question types, can be used to assess **any** of the issues. Look back to page 6 and read what you have to do to answer a 'How fully ...' type question.

Source E is from *Scotland's Relations with England* (1977) by William Ferguson.

> As it was, once the contents of the treaty had been leaked, nearly every sector of the Scottish nation found something objectionable in the proposed union. The Jacobites, rightly enough from their standpoint, saw it as a deadly blow to the hopes of the exiled Stuarts. The Episcopalians, most of whom favoured the Stuarts, were afraid that the union would secure Presbyterianism. The Presbyterians welcomed the Protestant succession, but feared that, under the union, bishops would again be thrust upon the Church of Scotland. Strangely, the offer of free trade gained little enthusiasm in many of the royal burghs, including Glasgow.

Question

How fully does source E explain feelings in Scotland towards the union up to 1740?

Use the source and recalled knowledge.

Writing your answer

Use the following advice to help write a fluent answer.

The source comments on Scottish feelings about union by using examples such as Jacobite resentment; Episcopalian fears; Presbyterian fears; and also worries about trade.

Write a brief paragraph on each of these examples and try to explain briefly feelings in Scotland towards the union up to 1740 (perhaps with quotes).

You should then use your own knowledge to write about feelings in Scotland towards union up to 1740. For example, information linked to the Jacobite rising of 1715 and also laws passed by the new British Parliament that seemed to hurt the Presbyterian church, such as the Toleration and Patronage Acts could be used as evidence.

How many marks would you give?

- Does the answer select information from the source and explain it briefly? You can give **up to** 4 marks for doing that.
- Does your answer provide a balance to the answer by using a lot of recall that is relevant to the question? You can give **up to** 7 marks for that.

When researching history topics for yourself, we recommend looking at the following websites:

- SCRAN (*www.scran.ac.uk*), a website run by the Royal Commission on the Ancient and Historical Monuments of Scotland, containing over 360,000 images and documents from museums and archives.
- Learning and Teaching Scotland's website (*www.ltscotland.org.uk/higherscottishhistory*), which has sections on all the units of Higher History.

Ypres
Loos
Cambrai
Somme
Verdun

Scotland on the eve of the Great War – the background

This section is about what Scotland was like just before the First World War broke out.

Issue 1 – Scots on the Western Front

This issue is about why so many Scots joined the army, and what they experienced on the Western Front.

Issue 2 – The effect of the war on life in Scotland

This issue deals with how the war affected the people of Scotland, and their way of life.

Issue 3 – How did the war affect Scottish industry and the economy?

This issue deals with what happened to Scotland's industries, Scottish workers and the Scottish economy during and after the war.

Issue 4 – How did the First World War affect Scottish politics?

This issue is about how the war made people think more about politics, how people became more political and what happened to the political parties.

Scotland after the war: a perspective

This section provides an opportunity to think about what the Great War meant to Scots and whether or not the war had any lasting effect on Scottish identity.

Scotland on the eve of the Great War – the background

There will be no questions in the exam about this first section, which is about what Scotland was like just before the First World War broke out.

To cover the syllabus you should know about the following:

- The strengths and weaknesses of the Scottish economy. Weaknesses in the economy were made worse by the effects of the Great War.
- What it was like to live in Scotland at that time, the differences between rural and urban Scotland and why so many Scots tried to escape from Scotland by emigrating.
- What the main differences between the political parties in Scotland were and why the Liberals were so strong in Scotland before 1914.
- Why Scottish soldiers were thought to be among the best fighting men in the world.

What was Scotland like in 1900?

In Scotland in 1900 just over half the population lived in cities, the other half living in rural communities. In cities such as Glasgow, Edinburgh, Dundee and Aberdeen many of the middle and upper classes lived in the suburbs and town houses. Meanwhile, most of the working classes lived in dark, smoky overcrowded conditions in the towns and cities. At the beginning of the 20th century 90% of Glaswegians shared a toilet with another family and 70% of its population lived in one- or two-roomed flats.

The drift of the rural population into cities looking for work increased the scale of urbanisation. By 1900 just over 10% of the working population still worked in farming. To escape poverty and seek opportunities elsewhere over half a million migrated from Scotland between 1904 and 1913. The preferred destinations were the USA, Canada, Australia and New Zealand.

At the same time, immigration to Scotland was also important. As well as tens of thousands of Irish who had settled mainly in the west of Scotland, new immigrants from Lithuania and Italy added to Scotland's population mix.

The Highlands continued to lose population. Historians still debate the effects of the Clearances and the impact of fashionable tourism on the Highlands in the late 19th century. Whether or not Highlanders were pushed by economic pressures or pulled by attractive opportunities elsewhere, the fact remains that the Highland population was falling.

The Napier Commission of the 1880s reported that many Highlanders were living in misery and poverty, and it was around this time that the roots of the Highland land problem were laid down. Later, during and after the First World War the unresolved problem of the 'land question' would return to haunt the government.

Scotland before 1914

Was Scotland the 'Workshop of the World' before 1914?

Around 1900 central Scotland was booming. The central belt of Scotland led the world in the production of coal, iron and steel, shipbuilding and engineering.

Between 1880 and 1914 coal was Scotland's fastest growing industry and in 1900 over 150 000 miners worked in Scotland's coalmines. By 1914 almost 20% of the world's shipping was built on the Clyde. Demand for steel created boom towns such as Airdrie, Coatbridge, Mossend and Wishaw. By 1911 Scottish steel towns were producing over one million tonnes each year.

Textile production was still a major employer. In Dundee over seventy jute mills employed tens of thousands of people, especially women.

The spread of railways allowed fresh fish to be transported across Britain with the result that many fishing ports, such as Eyemouth, began to prosper.

Were there problems with Scotland's economy before 1914?

There were signs that all was not well with the Scottish and British economies before 1914. The Scottish economy relied on overseas markets: international trade was vital.

However, there was a lack of new investment in Scottish industries. In the case of coal mining, new industries such as oil, gas production and electricity cut demand for coal in people's homes. Foreign competition took away markets. Mine owners were slow to invest in new, more efficient technology.

Scotland's heavy industries were all interlinked. Each was dependent on the other's success. That was one of the causes of Scotland's difficulties after the Great War.

By 1914 it was clear that the world was buying less from Scotland. If trade was disrupted and export markets were lost, the Scottish economy would suffer. For example, shipbuilding depended heavily on international trade, carrying Scottish exports around the world.

Why was the Liberal Party so popular in Scotland before the Great War?

The Liberals dominated Scottish politics before 1914. The other parties – the Conservatives, the Labour Party and the Unionists – posed no real threat to them. In 1910, the Liberals won fifty-seven out of seventy Scottish seats.

There were several reasons why so many voters supported the Liberals. The Liberals claimed to represent the best interests of working-class and middle-class men. Liberals were against big landowners, and that won them votes in the Highlands. Liberals also supported new laws to help people who were poor through no fault of their own. Liberal social reforms between 1906 and 1911 helped the young, the old, the sick and the unemployed.

What was unionism and who were Unionists?

Unionists were people who supported the union of Scotland, England, Ireland and Wales and were opposed to any attempt to break it up. In the 1880s, Liberal Prime Minister William Gladstone proposed that Ireland should have Home Rule, which meant that Ireland should rule itself. The immediate effect on the Liberals was damaging. The party split, with many of the older, more traditional, Liberals breaking away to form the Liberal Unionists. Liberal Unionists and Conservatives joined together to create the Scottish Unionist Party in 1912.

Why were the Conservatives unpopular?

The Conservatives were associated with the big landowners and landlords in the towns, who in turn were seen to be making huge profits from rents charged for poor quality housing.

Conservatives (sometimes called Tories) also supported a policy called protection. Protection meant putting up tariff barriers to protect British farming against foreign competition. The effect would be to make food from abroad more expensive. In Scotland protection was not popular. The urban population did not want food prices to rise and Scottish industries did not want anything that would make trade more difficult. For all those reasons, Conservative policies were not widely popular in Scotland.

How important was the Labour Party in Scotland before 1914?

The Labour Party was very new and untested before 1914. The party failed to make any big impression in Scotland before the First World War, with only three Scottish Labour MPs from a British total of forty-two Labour MPs in 1910. In 1914 the Labour Party did not seem to be very important.

How did Scots see themselves within the union of the UK?

Most Scots thought of themselves as British and were happy to be part of Britain and its empire. There was almost no support for Scottish nationalism and the Scottish National Party did not exist. Scots saw themselves as equal partners with the English as soldiers, statesmen, engineers and businessmen.

What is meant by Scotland's martial traditions?

From the middle of the 18th century the British government was keen to recruit Highlanders into the British army. The 'kiltie' soldier came to represent the brave heroes in popular magazines and stories that helped win the empire for Britain and defeated Britain's enemies.

As the empire grew, so did the need for soldiers. Highland landowners were only too happy to take advantage of government incentives to recruit men from their estates. When war broke out in 1914 the recruitment drive often made young Scottish men feel pressurised into believing they should not let down their ancestors and Scotland's martial, or military, traditions.

Issue 1 – Scots on the Western Front

This issue is about why so many Scots joined the army, and what they experienced on the Western Front.

To cover the syllabus you should know about the following:

- How Scots were persuaded to join the army when war broke out.
- What life in the trenches was like for Scottish soldiers.
- Why the battles of Loos and the Somme meant so much to Scotland.
- How important Scottish soldiers were to the overall war effort.

Why did Britain get involved in a European war?

On 4 August 1914 Britain joined the Great War.

Tensions in Europe had been building for some time. By 1914 European powers were divided into competing alliances, often described as two armed camps. On one side was the Triple Alliance of Germany, Austria-Hungary and Italy. They faced the Triple Entente of France, Russia and Great Britain.

Britain had no recent alliances. It did have friendly agreements with France and Russia, but that was all. Britain clung to the belief that it was safe, as an island protected by its huge Dreadnought battleships.

The assassination of Archduke Franz Ferdinand in Sarajevo on 28 June 1914 led eventually to war between Austria-Hungary and Russia by the end of July 1914. The snowball of alliances then started rolling and within a few days most of Europe was at war. Once Germany declared its support for Austria-Hungary, France declared its support for Russia. Germany, facing the prospect of fighting both France and Russia, launched its Schlieffen Plan. The Schlieffen Plan aimed to launch a massive attack through neutral Belgium, defeat an unprepared France and then send all German forces to attack Russia – all within six weeks.

The Schlieffen Plan aimed to launch a massive attack through neutral Belgium, defeat an unprepared France and then send all German forces to attack Russia – all within six weeks. The Schlieffen Plan failed, mainly because of a miscalculation by the Germans over the issue of invading Belgium. In 1839, Britain, along with other European powers, had signed the Treaty of London. It guaranteed the neutrality of Belgium. The Kaiser did not believe any country would bother about the Treaty of London, referring to it as a 'scrap of paper'. However, Britain did decide to support Belgium, and on 4 August 1914 Britain declared war on Germany. In reality the invasion of Belgium provided Britain with the excuse it had been looking for to get involved in the war and 'teach Germany a lesson'.

Why did Britain need to increase the size of its army quickly?

When war broke out in August 1914, the British government expected a short war, hopefully 'over by Christmas'. The British government did not expect to fight a land-based European war. Britain had not been involved in a large-scale war on mainland Europe for a hundred years. The British government expected that its navy would protect Britain and its empire, and thought that any fighting in Europe would be carried out by its friends, Russia and France.

Members of the government were therefore shocked when the new Secretary of State for War, Field-Marshal Lord Kitchener, stated that Britain would need a million men to defeat Germany and that it would take at least three years to do it.

The British Expeditionary Force (BEF) was the title given to the forces of the British army sent from Great Britain to fight in France and Belgium in the opening months of the First World War. In comparison to all other European armies the BEF was tiny. The BEF began moving across to France on Monday, 10 August, 1914 and by the end of the year the BEF had suffered so many casualties that there was a danger that Britain would be unable to keep fighting. The problem facing the British army now was to train and equip men fast enough so they could replace the casualties suffered by the BEF.

How were Scots persuaded to join the army?

Kitchener recruitment poster

Kitchener immediately began a recruiting campaign by calling for men aged between nineteen and thirty to join the British army. Three weeks later Kitchener raised the maximum recruiting age to thirty-five.

Recruitment posters could be seen everywhere. All across Scotland and Britain, young men were being urged to join the army through a mixture of peer pressure, guilt, appeals to patriotism and by suggesting that joining the army would provide an exciting life of adventure.

Kitchener stated, 'I feel certain that Scotsmen have only to know that their country urgently needs their service for them to offer [join up] with the same splendid patriotism as they have always shown in the past.'

Kitchener was right – his campaign was a huge success. More Scots volunteered in proportion to the size of the population than any other area of the UK. By the end of August, 20 000 men from the Glasgow area had joined up. The number of volunteers was far more than even Kitchener had hoped for.

There are many different reasons why so many young Scottish men joined the army in a sudden rush during late summer 1914. Certainly the virtues of heroism, self-sacrifice, honour and patriotism played a big part. Some young men thought they would look good in a kilt. Others wanted to escape the boredom and drudgery of their work and their lives. The attraction of adventure and excitement was strong. In Scotland, there was a traditional respect for the military and, for those who were unemployed or unskilled, the army offered a steady wage. Even after the casualty lists lengthened in 1915, recruitment in Scotland remained higher than many other parts of Britain.

In England a system of recruitment called 'Pals Battalions' was started. The 'Pals Battalions' were units of the British army that consisted of men who had volunteered together, with the promise that they would be able to serve alongside their mates rather than being scattered in different units of the army.

In Scotland there were no official 'Pals Battalions' but in reality they did exist. Although the name 'Pals Battalion' was not officially recognised in Scotland, the idea that volunteers who joined together would stay together operated. In Glasgow four battalions of men were raised and in Edinburgh there were three.

In Glasgow, the 15th (City of Glasgow) Battalion of the Highland Light Infantry was known as the Tramway Battalion. Most of the volunteers had worked in the city's transport department. At first the men of the Tramway Battalion had no uniform to wear so they wore their green tramway uniforms as they marched through the city. Another locally raised battalion in Glasgow was the 16th Battalion, known as the Boys' Brigade Battalion because most of the volunteers had been in the BBs.

In Edinburgh, Cranston's Battalion and McCrae's Battalion were raised from local men and became part of the Royal Scots. McCrae's Battalion was the most famous because of its connection with Hearts football club. The entire first and reserve team players, several boardroom and staff members and many supporters all joined McCrae's Battalion.

The idea of friends going to war together had many attractions, but it was also a recipe for disaster. Nobody seems to have thought what would happen if a Pals Battalion went into action and suffered heavy casualties. The effect on the area the Pals came from would be devastating.

Why did the Western Front get bogged down in trench warfare so quickly?

When war broke out some military planners expected the war to be over around Christmas time after a few decisive battles. Only General Kitchener thought differently. He told the prime minister that it would take at least three years to defeat Germany, at the cost of millions of casualties.

When the BEF arrived in France they advanced towards the German forces. At Mons the BEF slowed the German advance but still had to retreat. The Germans pushed on but soon the Schlieffen Plan began to unravel. Belgian resistance and the actions of the BEF caused the German advance to become disorganised. At the River Marne the BEF and the French army stopped the German advance. French and British troops forced Germans to retreat. The Schlieffen Plan had failed.

The Germans retreated until they found good defensive positions where they could 'dig in' and build defensive trenches. A basic trench was simply a deep ditch dug by soldiers to protect themselves and also to make it easier to defend their position.

Naturally, when British and French forces met the German defences, they too dug trenches to protect themselves. Each side tried to break through and outflank their enemy but all that happened was that each side dug more trenches and widened their defensive front. Eventually both sides had dug defensive lines stretching over 600 miles from the English Channel to the Swiss border. As the winter dragged on into 1915 the Western Front became bogged down in trench warfare. Each side pounded the other with artillery but that just ravaged the landscape, making it very difficult to attack over. Barbed wire and machine-gun fire made defence relatively easy and attack much more difficult.

For most of the next four years neither side managed a decisive breakthrough.

What was trench warfare like?

Letters home from soldiers all report living with noise, itching, boredom and mud. Most letters do not describe the possibility of death at any moment from a mortar shell or sniper fire.

However, soldiers did not live in the trenches throughout the war, week after week. Most Scottish soldiers were used in a rotation system. Usually, if a 'Jock' (a Scottish soldier) was in a front line trench on a Monday he would be 'rotated' back to a reserve and then rest and recovery position by the following weekend. Of course, by the next weekend he would have been in reserve and then be back into the front line again.

When troops were moved back from the front line, uniforms were debugged of lice, washed, ironed and exchanged if too badly infested. Nevertheless, the truth is that thousands of soldiers were eating, sleeping, fighting and dying in muddy holes in the ground. As the war dragged on, soldiers realised the war would not be over by Christmas, nor probably by the next Christmas either.

The problem with a deadlock is that something has to be done to try to break through. On the Western Front that meant troops would be sent 'over the top' in attempts to break the enemy trenches. Until 1918 these frontal assaults almost always resulted in fearful casualty numbers. One soldier, Douglas Hepburn of the London Scottish, wrote to his mother that,

> The Germans at the point where we attacked were ready and too strong for us... the machine gun was turned on us and therefore the casualties increased. In the morning we saw all the dead bodies lying about in different positions, all our own men of course, especially just in front of the Germans' barbed wire.

Letters from the front line were censored, partly to prevent the enemy learning information that might help them but partly also to keep up morale back home. One soldier from Aberdeen wrote that his officer had failed to send his letter home because he thought the letter might alarm some of the people there. The soldier wrote in his diary, 'They're not worth fighting for if they are so easily alarmed.'

The battle of Loos

Why is the battle of Loos called a Scottish battle?

In September 1915, 35 000 Scots took part in an attack, and half of the seventy-two infantry battalions that took part in the battle had Scottish names. Out of the 21 000 dead over 7000 were Scottish soldiers. Almost every town and village in Scotland was affected by the losses at Loos.

Why was the battle of Loos fought?

In September 1915, an attack began near the Belgian town of Loos. British commanders did not want to attack then or there, as they knew Kitchener's New Armies were not yet fully trained. The commanders wanted to wait until 1916 before launching these new armies into the attack. General Haig also had serious worries about the area of attack. He knew attacking soldiers would have almost no cover and would be in full view of German machine-gunners.

The French still wanted the British attack to go ahead and appealed directly to Kitchener who himself was under pressure to do all he could to encourage British and French cooperation. He agreed the attack should go ahead.

Haig planned to attack with six divisions, three of which were Scottish. Loos was the first time Kitchener's armies of volunteers had been used in a major attack. It was also the first time the British army used poison gas as a weapon. Haig planned to release chlorine from canisters but these canisters depended on a steady wind blowing towards the Germans.

There is some confusion about how effective the gas attack was. Some reports suggest the wind changed and blew the gas back in the faces of the attacking Scots. In many parts of the battlefield the Germans were pushed back but casualties were enormous. Reinforcements were needed but they were slow to arrive. By the time the attack was resumed, German reinforcements had arrived; the British attack had lost the element of surprise; they had no gas cover and the Germans were waiting for them. Once the attack began the German machine-guns cut down the men from Kitchener's army in their thousands.

Why is the battle of Loos called a Scottish battle?

In September 1915, 35 000 Scots took part in the attack at Loos. Although officially the battle of Loos continued until 18 October 1915, in effect it finished after just three days. Battalions from every Scottish regiment fought in the battle of Loos. Half of the seventy-two infantry battalions that took part in the battle had Scottish names. Out of the 21 000 dead over 7000 were Scottish soldiers. Almost every town and village in Scotland was affected by the losses at Loos.

One longer-term result of the failure at Loos was that Sir John French was replaced as commander of the BEF by Douglas Haig. Haig was in charge of the British 1st army and he expressed his concern about the suitability of an attack at Loos. However Haig's concerns were overruled by Kitchener who said the attack as planned was vital for British-French cooperation. When the battle was over, Haig lost no time in reminding Kitchener of his reservations and also pinned most of the blame on the commander of the BEF, Sir John French. Four days after the end of the battle, a letter from Haig to Kitchener blamed French for indecision in sending in reserve troops and for using Kitchener's New Army of volunteers before the were 'battle ready'. Haig wrote, 'My attack was a complete success' but then blamed French as Commander in Chief in charge of the reserve divisions for sending them into battle too late. Haig ended by writing, 'I feel annoyed at the lost opportunity'. (NA/PRO 30/57/50 Kitchener Papers Haig to Kitchener September 29,1915.) Within days French was sacked and Haig was promoted to the top job of Commander in Chief of the BEF.

The following year, 1916 Haig led British forces into the battle that will forever be linked to his name - the Battle of the Somme.

Why was the battle of the Somme fought?

The battle of the Somme started on 1 July 1916. It was fought for two main reasons – to divert German forces away from the battle of Verdun, where French forces were suffering huge casualties and, secondly, to inflict high casualties on the German army.

Three full Scottish divisions took part and many Scottish battalions also fought in other divisions. Those soldiers and the public back home were told the Somme had much bigger objectives. Propaganda declared the attack on the Somme was the 'big push' that would lead to victory.

What was attrition?

General Douglas Haig had replaced Sir John French as military commander at the end of 1915. Haig argued that making the enemy fight and wearing them down man by man and bullet by bullet would make defeat for Germany inevitable. Haig's policy was called attrition. It meant accepting high British casualties in the knowledge that Britain had greater resources than Germany to fight a long war. Haig believed that eventually Germany would no longer have enough men or equipment to keep fighting.

Why did the Somme result in such high casualties?

Haig planned to batter the enemy lines with a five-day-long artillery barrage (increased to seven days because of bad weather) that would destroy the Germans' barbed wire, wreck their trenches and kill the German defenders. In reality, the barrage failed to do its job. Just before troops went over the top, patrols reported that the enemy front line was strongly held. Too many shrapnel shells were used that simply threw the German barbed wire up in the air and let it fall in a worse tangle than before. Many other British shells had failed to explode. To make matters worse, German machine-gun crews had been sheltering deep underground away from the artillery blasts. When the artillery barrage eventually stopped the German machine-gunners put their practice drill into operation. They were out of their shelters and ready to fire within two minutes.

When the British attack began at 7.30 a.m. and the waves of British Tommies went over the top, they were met by deadly machine-gun and mortar fire. One report written at the time by the Scottish author John Buchan described how the British troops moved forward in line after line but minute by minute the lines melted away, destroyed by high explosives, shrapnel, rifle and machine-gun fire.

On the first day of the battle the British suffered their highest ever casualties – almost 60 000 dead, wounded or missing. Most of the casualties were taken before the first hundred metres had been crossed.

What had gone wrong?

Many reasons have been put forward to explain the slaughter on the Somme.

The Germans had, for some time, been strengthening their defences in the area, digging especially deep concrete shelters. German machine-gun teams therefore survived the bombardment and were ready to fire as troops advanced over No Man's Land. The bombardment itself had failed to knock out the German artillery and in many places the shells had failed to cut the German barbed wire.

The battle of the Somme has been described as the graveyard of Kitchener's armies and also of the various Pals Battalions. On the Somme, the 16th Battalion, Highland Light Infantry (the Boys' Brigade Battalion) suffered more than 500 casualties. The deaths of so many young men from the same background devastated the close-knit communities back home. The same could be said for Cranston's and McCrae's Battalions of the Royal Scots, which suffered 75% casualties. After the losses on the Somme, and particularly once conscription was introduced, all thoughts of keeping Pals Battalions together were abandoned.

After two days, the survivors of the first assault battalions had been moved back to the rear to recover and new battalions were sent out to carry on the attack. However, fresh attacks just added to the casualty lists. On 14 July a second phase of the battle started and the 51st Highland Division lost 3500 men attacking High Wood. The first day of the new assault cost 9000 British lives.

What were the results of the battle of the Somme?

After the war German commanders described the battle of the Somme as 'the muddy grave of the German army'. In the long run the British army could replace its losses. The empire and, by 1917, the USA stood behind Britain. However, Germany had no allies ready to send fresh troops and no future hope of fresh resources.

Overall 400 000 British soldiers lost their lives on the Somme but the battle had eased the pressure on the French at Verdun and it cost the Germans almost as many men as the British. Only later did it become clear that the battle of the Somme had broken the back of the German army on the Western Front.

The leadership of Douglas Haig – does he deserve praise or criticism?

For most people Douglas Haig, commander of British forces on the Western Front from December 1915 until the end of the war, is the man most closely associated with the casualty figures on the Western Front. Some people believe Haig was responsible for the high casualties, others believe that Haig was the man who won the war for Britain.

Haig was born in Edinburgh into the wealthy Haig whisky-making family. In August 1914, when the war started, Haig was the general commanding the First Army Corps. On Christmas Day 1914, Haig was given command of the First Army – the army he led at the battle of Loos. The failure to break through at Loos and the argument over the control of reserves led eventually to Haig replacing Sir John French as Commander-in-Chief. Haig then remained as commander of the BEF until the end of the war.

What are the relevant facts to think about when assessing Haig's strategy?

At the end of the war the public were shocked by the huge casualty figures. At the time, many grieving relatives blamed Haig for the slaughter on the Western Front. Later, some historians have continued to blame Haig for his insensitivity to the mounting casualty figures. How fair is that criticism?

When reaching a conclusion about Haig's failings as a military commander and his responsibility for the high casualty figures, the following points should be considered

- When Haig became Commander-in-Chief the Western Front was already in deadlock.
- Haig was ordered to push the German armies out of French and Belgian territory.
- Haig was ordered to cooperate closely with French forces. In 1916 Haig was under pressure from the British government and the French to launch an attack on the Somme to relieve pressure on the French armies.
- The new armies raised by the Kitchener recruitment schemes were untested in war and, in some cases, only trained to a very basic standard. Haig wanted more time to prepare his new armies of volunteers but he was overruled.
- If Haig had halted the Somme attack on 2 July, what would have been gained? Lack of British cooperation would have angered the French and perhaps risked the alliance.
- The attack on the Somme cost many thousands of German lives and it can be argued that the attrition of the Somme was the beginning of the end for the German army.
- Haig did encourage the use of new technology where available and appropriate. The technology available to generals in 1918 was not there in 1914 or even 1916. Haig had asked for 150 tanks to use at the Somme but only 50 arrived and half of them became unusable. New thinking, new armies and new technology, all under the direction of Haig, led to the victory of 1918.
- Haig and his organisation of the army turned thousands of ordinary civilians into an efficient modern army and led them to victory in 1918.
- By 1918 Haig had fought and defeated the enemy in the main theatre of war – Western Europe. By 1918 Haig had broken the deadlock on the Western Front.
- The public image of Haig as a man who cared nothing about casualties was created to a large extent by the memoirs of wartime Prime Minister Lloyd-George, a man who hated Haig. The memoirs contained things said by Haig yet taken out of context to create a very negative impression of him such as, 'The machine-gun is a much overrated weapon' and 'The nation must be taught to bear losses'.
- After the war Haig was a central figure in the creation of the British Legion and the Earl Haig Fund, both of which were founded to help ex-servicemen.
- Critics of Haig say that he 'won the war' only because the German army was exhausted by 1918. Yet the German army was still able to inflict 380 000 casualties on the Allied forces between August and November 1918. The German army did not fade away. Haig defeated it.

Memorial poppy wreath

Issue 2 – The effect of the war on life in Scotland

This issue deals with how the war affected the people of Scotland and their way of life.

To cover the syllabus you should know about the following:

- What DORA was and why some Scots objected to it.
- What conscription was and why it started.
- What conscientious objectors were and why they were against conscription.
- How the war affected women in Scotland.
- How Scotland coped with the size of its losses in the war.

DORA, censorship and government control of the Home Front

What was DORA?

DORA was the short name for the Defence of the Realm Act that became law on 8 August 1914. It was a law that allowed the government to pass many new measures to protect the country during the war.

One of the first security worries when war broke out was the risk of spies. The government needed to secure all transport networks from acts of sabotage, such as blowing up railway tracks or setting fire to timber yards. Spy stories in newspapers warned the public to watch out for any suspicious-looking people.

DORA also increased censorship in newspapers. At that time there were no public radio or television broadcasts to worry about. Reports about the war in newspapers were written to give a very positive slant or bias in favour of British forces while reports about the Germans were intended to make people hate them. In other words, most war reporting was propaganda and was seldom allowed to tell the whole truth. Even letters home from front-line soldiers were censored so as not to worry the folks at home or give help to the enemy. It was always possible spies could intercept letters and gain valuable information!

Why did opposition to DORA increase during the war?

At first the public accepted the need for increased security and control over things that were seen to be vital for the war effort. However, as the war went on, the public became tired of restrictions that seemed only to have a slight connection with the war effort.

When DORA was used to help war production by limiting the opening times of pubs and reducing the alcoholic strength of beer, many people objected. Some people even had to give up their homing pigeons when the authorities feared the birds might be used to send messages to Germans. Police were on the watch for anyone whistling at night in case they were signalling to low flying Zeppelin air ships overhead!

More seriously, people objected to the way that DORA was undermining civil liberties. Critics of DORA felt the government was abusing its powers and silencing legitimate political debate, including anti-war opinion. DORA also gave the government the right to imprison people without trial, and that was directly against the freedoms that British people had struggled to win over many years.

There was also discontent at the way the government claimed that any anti-government protest was against Britain's war effort and was therefore not patriotic. Public protest against DORA was therefore confused in many people's minds with helping the Germans in some way.

One example of how the government used DORA to turn legitimate protest into an unpatriotic act was in the reporting of strikes on Clydeside in 1915. The government shut down anti-government newspapers such as *Forward* for a short time while pro-government reporting tried to show the strikers as undermining the war effort and threatening the lives of soldiers on the front line.

Criticism of DORA increased when conscription started (see pages 90–91). Under the conscription laws, men could be conscripted (or forced) to serve in the armed forces or do jobs of national importance. For civilians on the Home Front, conscription meant that conscripted workers were no longer civilians. They were under military authority and discipline and as such were denied the right to strike.

Conscription had not been used in Britain before and its introduction was seen by some as yet another increase in the power of the state at the cost of individual liberty.

Did most people object to DORA?

No, they did not. The public believed government action was necessary to win the war. In 1914 Prime Minister Asquith had been criticised for saying life in Britain during the war was 'business as usual'. By 1915 everyone knew that was nonsense. The war required a huge effort from everyone to win it so DORA was seen as the way the government could direct and control the war effort necessary for victory.

Did everyone support the war?

When war broke out thousands of young Scots rushed to join up and 'do their bit'. However, not everyone supported the war effort. Some did not believe the propaganda that was meant to create anti-German feeling and stoke up a 'war fever'. There were many people in Scotland who opposed the war, did not wish to volunteer and then resisted conscription.

The strongest political group to oppose the war was the Independent Labour Party (ILP), which immediately attacked the official Labour Party's support for Kitchener's recruitment campaign. The ILP's newspaper called *Forward* was often criticised and even closed down for its persistent attacks on government policy. In the pro-war atmosphere of autumn 1914 any voice that asked for compromise and rational thought about how to stop the war was shouted down as unpatriotic and a threat to Britain's safety.

Anti-war opinion was not popular. In the first two weeks of the war Britain suffered 20 000 casualties. Nevertheless, the ILP and other socialists continued to protest against the war. By the end of 1914, ILP membership had fallen to 3000 and the party was described as a pacifist group that threatened to dampen the war enthusiasm of the nation.

What was the UDC?

The Union of Democratic Control was another organisation that opposed conscription and wartime censorship along with other restrictions on civil liberties. The UDC was not linked to any one political party but as both the Liberal and Conservative parties actively supported the war, the UDC became dominated by left-wing Liberal and Labour activists. Scottish political figures such as Ramsay MacDonald, Tom Johnston and David Kirkwood were members of the UDC and became well known for their radical policies and actions during the war.

By 1915 the Union of Democratic Control had 300 000 members and was the most important of all the anti-war organisations in Britain. Members of the UDC were under constant threat from members of the public who believed the UDC was a cover organisation for supporters of Germany during the war – in other words, traitors. The *Daily Express* suggested that the UDC was working for the German government. It published details of future UDC meetings and encouraged its readers to go and break them up.

By the end of the war the UDC still had over 10 000 members, showing that public opinion did not always support the war, despite what government propaganda would have liked the people to believe. In 1924 several members of the UDC were in the new Labour government that was elected in that year.

Why was conscription started in Britain?

Britain was the only army in 1914 that was made up entirely of volunteers. Every other country used conscription to swell its armies. Conscription meant that young men had no choice but to join the armed forces for some time. There they were trained and when they returned to civilian life after two years they remained on reserve. As 'reservists' they could be called up in an emergency. In August 1914 these reservists were being called up to swell all the armies of Europe apart from Britain.

Only in Britain did the army rely on volunteers. However, even before war broke out the UK Parliament had debated the issue of conscription at least four times. Supporters of conscription argued that young men had a duty above all else to defend their country. When the voluntary recruitment rate seemed to fall after the initial rush in the late summer of 1914, the calls to introduce conscription became louder.

What was done to resist conscription?

In 1914 Clifford Allen and Fenner Brockway started an organisation in England called the No Conscription Fellowship. By early 1915 a Glasgow branch of the NCF had been formed. Later that same year the NCF had spread across Scotland. The ILP was also against conscription and both organisations were jointly condemned in the popular newspapers as cowardly, and undermining Britain's war effort. In Scotland, it has been claimed that almost 70% of all objectors were members of the ILP.

In January 1916, the Military Service Act brought in conscription for single men from nineteen to forty years old. In May 1916 conscription was extended to married men and by 1918 men up to the age of fifty were being conscripted.

The Military Service Act of 1916 made allowances for certain men to be exempt (excused) from military service. Apart from men who were physically or mentally unfit for service, there were three main categories that would allow men to be exempt from conscription.

- The first category exempted men involved in work of national importance to the war effort. Many coal miners, for example, were excused military service.
- The second category exempted men if their service in the armed forces would cause 'serious hardship owing to his exceptional financial or business obligations or domestic position'.
- The third category included young men who refused to fight on grounds of their conscience. These 'conscientious objectors', or 'conchies' for short, claimed exemption on grounds of their political or religious beliefs.

What happened to conscientious objectors?

Conscientious objectors were taken to a military tribunal. These tribunals were like military courts and made up from local people, such as businessmen, landowners or shopkeepers, and also included one representative from the military.

The objections of the 'conchies' were listened to, usually not very sympathetically, and a decision was taken as to whether or not to accept the reasons for conscientious objection. The intention of the tribunal was to conscript as many men as possible into the armed forces so the reasons of the conchies were usually rejected.

About 16 000 men across the UK refused to fight. Most of these men were pacifists who believed that it was wrong to kill another human being. Such conscientious objectors were provided with alternatives to armed service.

Around 7000 conscientious objectors agreed to perform non-combat duties, often as stretcher-bearers the front line. However, more than 1500 pacifists refused all military service. They argued their role within the war effort would release other soldiers into combat roles so they would be fighting 'by proxy'. These 'absolutists' opposed undertaking any work whatsoever that helped Britain's war effort. As a result, absolutists were usually imprisoned.

There were also 'alternativists' who were prepared to take on civilian work but not supervised by the military. Many Scots socialists took this choice rather than go to prison, arguing that inside prison their message would not be heard.

Across the UK 5970 conscientious objectors were court-martialled and sent to prison. Conditions were harsh. At least seventy-three conscientious objectors died because of the treatment they received.

Religious groups were divided over the issue of conscientious objectors. The big Church groups supported the war effort and it was difficult for individual Church leaders to speak out in parishes suffering the losses of their young men.

When the war ended the whole issue of the increase in the powers of the state over its citizens was far from over. In particular, the ILP campaigned for the repeal of the Military Service Act and the release of all conscientious objectors from prison. In May 1919, the longest-serving prisoners began to be released and by August the last conscientious objector was released. Many returned to civilian life to find that their families often shunned them, employers refused to offer jobs and Parliament tried to deny those who had refused non-combatant service the right to vote for five years.

Compulsory military conscription was finally abolished in December 1920.

Throughout the war the ILP had remained consistently opposed to the conflict and by 1918 many thousands of ordinary Scots had listened to the ILP's anti-war message. On the other hand, it is important to remember that compared to the millions who were directly involved in the war effort, the pacifists and war resisters were a tiny group of people; less than half of 1% of the population.

How did the war affect the lives and work of women in Scotland?

The Great War is often seen as a major turning point in the role of women in British society. The war opened up jobs to women that would otherwise have been closed to them and in 1918 some women were given the vote in national elections for the first time.

However, the question of how far the war caused a complete change in male attitudes to women is open to debate.

How were women's roles in society changing before 1914?

Male prejudices about 'a woman's place' had already begun to weaken. Before 1914 some women gained access to better education and also to some jobs in the professions. New laws had improved the legal rights of women.

However, women still had no vote and those who campaigned for suffrage (the right to vote) argued that only by winning the vote could they significantly improve their lives and status in society.

In 1897, several local women's suffrage societies united to form the National Union of Women's Suffrage Societies. These women believed in moderate, 'peaceful' tactics to win the vote, mainly for middle class property owning women. Later the NUWSS was nicknamed the suffragists in contrast to the later suffragettes, the popular name for the members of the Women's Social and Political Union. Emmeline Pankhurst formed the WSPU in 1903. She was frustrated by the lack of progress achieved by the NUWSS.

At first, the suffragettes demonstrated peacefully, with rallies and processions, but by 1910 the suffragette campaign turned to more violent tactics. As a result more and more suffragettes were arrested and by the summer of 1914 over 1000 suffragettes were in prison.

When Britain declared war on Germany in August 1914 the government released all WSPU prisoners in order to encourage the suffragettes to end their campaign. In response, the WSPU agreed to stop their campaign and began a new pro-war propaganda campaign encouraging men to join the armed forces and women to demand 'the right to serve'.

How did women contribute to the war effort?

As casualty rates increased on the battlefield, and as conscription was introduced to swell the ranks, women were needed to fill the gaps in the workforce left by men who went off to fight.

Industries that had previously excluded women now welcomed them. Women worked as conductors on trams and buses, as typists and secretaries in offices and factories, and nearly 200 000 women found work in government departments. Thousands worked on farms in the land army, at the docks and even in the police. Some women, such as nurses, filled more traditional jobs. During the war nurses such as Mairi Chisholm became important role models for women eager to feel they were 'doing their bit' for the war effort.

Scots girl Mairi Chisholm was 18 in 1914 when she joined an experimental first aid post just behind the front line in Belgium. British authorities would not allow women so close to the fighting but the Belgian authorities had no such objections.

By working so close to the front line the women were in constant danger. In March 1918, Chisholm and the other nurses were affected by poison gas released against troops and although Chisholm recovered and returned to her post, she was never again fully fit.

Mairi Chisholm has only become well known in Scotland in recent years; much better known is the work of Elsie Inglis, another Scot who used her medical skills to assist in the war effort.

Elsie Inglis was the driving force in the creation of the Scottish Women's Hospitals Committee that sent over 1000 women doctors, nurses, orderlies and drivers to war zones across Europe and the

Balkans. Inglis was also involved in setting up four Scottish Women's Hospitals, which had much lower levels of death from disease than the more traditional military hospitals.

Having endured terrible conditions, capture, repatriation, and also fighting against male-dominated decision-making in the UK, Elsie Inglis eventually died from cancer in November 1917.

Elsie Inglis

Women and 'men's work'

Why were women not welcomed in many engineering factories?

By 1916 it was clear that women had become a vital part of the war effort. The biggest increase in female employment was in the previously male-dominated engineering industry, especially the part that made munitions.

Munitions meant every type of explosive artillery shell or bullet made for the war effort. The munitions factories were dangerous and unpleasant, with women working around the clock with explosive mixtures described as the 'devil's porridge'. In all, sixty-one British workers died from poisoning and seventy-one were killed by explosions. (69 of these deaths occured in one explosion in east London; 1 occurred at Gretna.)

Before the war, fewer than 4000 women worked in heavy industry in Scotland. By 1917 over 30 000 women were employed during the war making munitions in Scotland.

At first, men working in the engineering factories were worried about their loss of status and the threat to their wages. The problem was called 'dilution'.

What was dilution?

Dilution meant the fear expressed by skilled men who had served a seven-year apprenticeship that their skills would be 'diluted' by quickly-trained women. Those men feared that working women would weaken threaten their skills, their status in the workforce, their wages and even their future employment.

How was the issue of dilution solved?

As the demand for more and more weapons and munitions grew, the need to find an answer to the dilution row became urgent. The Ministry of Munitions introduced a dilution scheme whereby skilled jobs were broken down into individual processes. A woman could then be trained in that process and be allowed to work while under supervision. That way many women could be trained in different processes so the job was done but the status and skill of the 'skilled man' was not undermined.

The Munitions of War Act of 1915 also suggested that women should be paid comparable rates to men but that seldom happened.

Women and the rent strikes

What does radicalisation mean?

The Great War is said to have made many Scots more politically aware. Another way of saying that is that people became radicalised. The radicalisation of Scottish politics is dealt with on page 101 but the rent strikes that started in and around Glasgow are perfect examples of people taking direct action to change or protect their way of life.

What was a rent strike?

Rent strikes were the refusal of people, mainly women, to pay high rents charged by landlords. In February 1915, Helen Crawfurd, Mary Barbour, Agnes Dollan and Jessie Stephens helped to form the Glasgow Women's Housing Association to resist rent rises and threatened evictions. In May 1915 the first rent strike began and soon about 25 000 tenants in Glasgow had joined the strike.

Rent strikes began to spread to other Scottish cities such as Aberdeen and Dundee. Landlords began to issue court orders and threaten the protestors with eviction, fines or prison. In response the women made it impossible for the authorities to evict tenants, by blocking access to their tenements.

Why did rent strikes start in and around Glasgow?

The Glasgow area was vital to the war effort. The shipyards and engineering factories were crucial in producing the weapons, the munitions and the machines that Britain needed to fight the war. As a result of the demand for workers, the population of the Glasgow area increased as people arrived to meet the demand for workers. Those new arrivals all needed somewhere to stay, and as a result demand for housing in and around Glasgow rocketed – and so did the rents that landlords charged.

Housing conditions were often bad but landlords did little to improve their properties. They knew that, as more and more people were looking for somewhere to live near to the large engineering factories, they could charge high rents for poor quality housing.

Soon ordinary people were being evicted from their tenement flats simply because they could not pay the rent that had increased by as much as 20%. The women of Glasgow were furious at this profiteering. (Profiteering means taking advantage of a situation to make money while other people suffer and can do little about the profiteers.) Landlords bullied and threatened the women to make them pay higher rents. There was a strong feeling that the landlords were taking advantage of the women, threatening them with eviction while their menfolk were away fighting in the war. Faced with rising food prices and now rising rents, some women decided to fight back.

Why was the government concerned about rent strikes?

On 17 November 1915 a mass demonstration in Glasgow's George Square worried the government. The radicalisation of the women had also inspired some men who now began to strike in sympathy with the women and to campaign for wage rises for themselves. The government was under pressure. The rent strikes had grown to the extent that they threatened wartime production of necessary machines and munitions.

The answer was the Rent Restriction Act. Rents were frozen at 1914 levels unless improvements had been made to the property. The strikers' demands had been met, protests and profiteering now declined and wartime production was maintained without disruption.

However, the strikers had learned an important lesson: that direct action could lead to positive results. The rent strikes of 1915 had a big impact on the radicalisation of many Scots, as you will find out later.

Did the war really change the image and status of working women?

When the war ended the majority of women did not keep their new wartime jobs. The Restoration of Pre-War Practices Act meant that returning soldiers were given back their jobs and with the closure of most munitions factories women workers were no longer needed.

Within a few years of the end of the war over 25% of all working women were back in domestic service – child-minding and doing housework. That total was more than before the war.

Commemoration and remembrance

How did Scotland react to the end of the war?

On the eleventh hour of the eleventh day of the eleventh month of 1918 the fighting stopped. An armistice came into effect and ever since then 11 November 1918 has been called 'Armistice Day'. In the years after the war the name 'Poppy Day' was also used for the same occasion.

Across Scotland news of Armistice Day was met with relief. That relief showed itself sometimes in wild parties, sometimes as private sadness.

How many Scots died in the Great War?

Every community in Scotland was affected. There is no absolutely correct total for the number of Scottish casualties in the Great War. The official figure given at the end of the war calculated that Scotland had suffered 74 000 dead, but soon after the end of the war campaigners for a national war memorial claimed the figure was over 100 000. What is not disputed is that of all the countries involved in the Great War, Scotland's casualty rate of 26% of its fighting forces was among the highest of all.

How did Scots commemorate their war dead?

To commemorate means to use a formal occasion to remember something or someone. After four years of war, the Scottish population needed time to grieve, take stock of their losses and find some way to mark the sacrifice of their loved ones.

By 1917 there was growing support for a national memorial and a decision was taken to create a UK memorial in London, later known as the Cenotaph, or 'empty tomb', as no soldier is actually buried under it. However, there was also a feeling that Scotland should have its own national war memorial to remember its war dead.

The idea of war memorials to commemorate the dead was not new. At the top of the Mound in Edinburgh, for example, there is a monument to the dead from the South African war of 1899. What was different in 1918 was the desire to share grief and loss on a national scale.

How was Scotland's National War Memorial created?

The man who was the force behind the creation of a Scottish National War Memorial was the Duke of Atholl. He summed up the feeling of the country when he said the Scottish nation would put up a memorial 'with its own hands in its own country and with its own money'.

Atholl's plan was for a monument to be built in Edinburgh Castle and he lost no time in promoting the Scottish case for a memorial. Atholl argued that since the soldiers who were garrisoned in the castle were soon to be moved out to new accommodation at Redford Barracks, there would be plenty of space within the castle to build a suitable memorial.

As the costs of the project increased, and opposition to the design of the proposed memorial grew, it seemed as if it would never happen, but finally the opening ceremony took place on 14 July 1927. Scotland's National War Memorial stands in Crown Square within Edinburgh Castle. However, it is a fairly small area, so veterans and relatives from all over Scotland and the Commonwealth crowded onto the esplanade of Edinburgh castle to witness the commemoration of Scotland's war dead.

As soon as the new memorial was declared open thousands of mourners laid their wreaths and floral tributes in Crown Square, turning the grey flagstones into a carpet of colour.

Who were Scotland's war dead?

The names of Scotland's war dead were written on Rolls of Honour, and those Rolls of Honour were placed inside a casket, a gift from the king and queen.

A decision had been taken that each name on the Rolls of Honour should belong to a member of the Armed Forces of the Crown or of the Merchant Navy who was either a Scotsman (either born in Scotland or had a Scottish-born parent) or who had served in a Scottish Regiment and was either killed in the war or who had died as a result of it. In later years that decision complicated the calculation of Scotland's war dead. For example, would a dead Australian soldier whose parents had emigrated from Scotland count as an Australian casualty or a Scottish one?

In the years that followed the Great War, towns and villages across Scotland built their own memorials to remember and commemorate their own losses.

For those whose loved ones were never found or lay in foreign fields the Imperial War Graves Commission created and cared for military cemeteries around the world. Over 600 of these cemeteries were near the line of the old Western Front in France and Flanders, and these places also became places of pilgrimage for Scottish families in the 1920s. Huge numbers of Scottish relatives of the dead paid their respects at the Menin Gate memorial in Ypres when it opened in 1928 as they did also at numerous other places such as Beaumont Hamel and Thiepval.

All these memorials had a common hope – that the dead had not died in vain and that the Great War really would be the war to end all wars.

Issue 3 – How did the war affect Scottish industry and the economy?

This issue deals with what happened to Scotland's industries, Scottish workers and the Scottish economy during and after the war.

To cover the syllabus you should know about the following:

- How the war gave a big boost to industries such as coal mining and shipbuilding – and what happened to them when the war ended.
- How the war affected fishing and farming in Scotland – and what happened to them after the war.
- How people coped with wartime shortages.
- What problems the Scottish economy faced after the war.
- What the 'land question' was in the Highlands and Islands, and whether it was resolved.

The effects of the war on Scottish industries

Did the war help Scotland's traditional heavy industries?

The answer is yes and no. In the short term the war provided a temporary boost for Scotland's industries.

Before the war, Scottish industry seemed to be doing well. However, Scotland relied too heavily on a handful of main industries. For example, 14% of the adult male working population of Scotland depended in some way on the shipbuilding industry for their weekly wages.

These old traditional industries faced serious problems in the years before the war, but the war years provided a big boost to their production. When war did break out, the main shipyards on the Clyde were in effect taken over by the Royal Navy to produce warships. In fact, just before the war the shipyards had been saved by the naval race as they helped to build the new Dreadnought class of battleship.

The war was a lifeline to Scotland's flagging industries in 1914. Coal, shipbuilding and the production of iron and steel were all in big demand during the war. However, the demand for production during the war years made the fall in demand feel worse when it came during the post-war years. The introduction of new technology and production methods such as automatic machinery and assembly-line production methods speeded up production during the war but also threatened jobs.

After the war the slump in international trade, the fall in orders for new ships and the use of new production methods all combined to force unemployment upwards.

How was the fishing industry affected?

At first the North Sea was almost closed to fishing. Although the restrictions on fishing were lifted when food supplies became scarce, many boats and crews found themselves serving as support to the navy as coastal patrols, members of the Royal Navy Volunteer Reserve or searching for floating explosives called mines.

In 1918 the fishing industry faced rising fuel costs and the need to repair and equip boats after war service. Although the fishing industry did recover after the war, revolution and post-war changes in Eastern Europe meant that traditional export markets in Germany, Eastern Europe and Russia were lost.

How did the war affect farming?

During the war years farmers and farming had to face changes. Many farmers made money out of the rising demand for food and animals. Scottish sheep farmers did well out of the war. By 1918 sheep prices were 60% higher than in 1914. In 1917 the government had bought all wool sheared from sheep in the country to supply the need for uniforms and army blankets. At the same time, the wages of skilled ploughmen and shepherds doubled.

Although the number of farm workers stayed much the same, the type of farm worker changed. During the war years many men left farming to 'join up'. They were replaced by women, boys and older men. Even prisoners and conscientious objectors were used as farm workers during the war.

The war gave a boost to mechanisation as many thousands of farm horses were taken away for the war effort.

In 1914 Britain bought much of its food from abroad. When Germany began to use its submarine fleet to sink merchant ships carrying supplies to Britain the government did two things. First, it began a propaganda campaign to reduce waste and produce more food. Secondly, it began to ration food supplies.

Rationing

Why was rationing started?

The aim of rationing was to conserve food supplies, ensure fair distribution and control rising prices. When German submarines began targeting all merchant ships carrying food to Britain a system of rationing became almost inevitable. As food became scarcer, prices went up. For the wealthy price rises were an inconvenience but for the poor expensive food meant long queues and less money to spend on other essentials. Eventually lack of food would lead to ill health and even severe malnutrition.

By the end of 1917, it was clear that Britain was facing serious food shortages. Panic-buying led to worse shortages and so in January 1918 the government began a system of rationing, so that everyone could be sure of a regular and sufficient food supply. An organised system of rationing could also control the prices of basic foods.

Full-scale rationing was in force in Scotland by April 1918. Sugar was the first item to be rationed and this was later followed by butcher meat. By the end of the war almost all foods were subject to price control by the government.

Was rationing successful?

Rationing did ensure fairer supplies of food at reasonable prices. However, the defeat of the U-boat campaign and the surrender of Germany by the end of 1918 meant that Britain did not have to endure serious hardships that would have tested the rationing system to its limits. Perhaps a fair point to make is that it was the Royal Navy's blockade of Germany that caused starvation in Germany. Lack of food and war materials were the main reasons for the defeat of Germany. Perhaps victory belonged to the country that could manage its shortages the best.

Case study: the jute industry

Why is the rise and fall of the jute business a good case study of how the war affected Scottish industry?

The jute industry is a good example of an industry that was facing some difficulties before the war but received a huge boost as a result of the war. After the war it then faced a rapid decline. Run-down machinery and a return to old-fashioned working habits were no match for the new industrial world that emerged from the Great War. Foreign competition forced down prices and took away export markets.

What is jute, and why was it so important?

The jute industry was based in Dundee. It employed thousands of people, with 25% of Dundee's male workers and 67% of the female workers dependent on the jute industry for their employment.

Jute is a fibre grown mostly in Bangladesh, which was then part of India and within the British Empire. The raw jute fibres were exported to Dundee and made into sacking cloth.

During the war, demand for jute soared as the need for more and more sacks for sandbags increased to over 6 million sacks in one month. Jute was also used for many other things, including feedbags for thousands of horses. In a world with no plastics, jute was **the** packing material.

However, the war years could only ever provide a temporary boom. The good times did not last. The demands of constant wartime production had put huge pressure on Dundee's factories and machines. When the war ended, the jute factories in Dundee were in need of fresh investment and repair.

Dundee businessmen should also shoulder some of the blame for the decline of the jute industry in Scotland. During the war, Dundee's jute industry was protected by a government ban on jute products being processed in Calcutta. After the war the ban was lifted. Even before the war some

Dundee businessmen had started to develop the jute industry in the Calcutta area, thereby cutting out Dundee's part in the business. When the war ended, those same businessmen were ready to undercut the prices charged for jute processed in Dundee. As world jute prices fell along with demand for jute-based products, Dundee suffered.

The 'land question' and emigration

What was the 'land question' in the Highlands of Scotland?

There is a custom among historians to use the word 'question' when they mean 'problem'. In the first section of this unit, outlining issues facing Scotland on the eve of war, it was stated that the unresolved problem of the 'land question' would return to haunt the government. It did.

The land question in the Highlands was about land ownership. Without ownership, the crofters of the Highlands had faced eviction for many years. The Crofters Act of 1886 put an end to the Highland Clearances by granting security of tenure to the crofters. That meant the crofters could not be evicted from land they rented on the sudden whim of the landowner. That security meant that crofters could build substantial permanent houses on their land and plan for the future. However, the Act failed to restore the lost land from which the crofters and their ancestors had been forcibly evicted over the previous century.

The failure of the Crofters Act to restore the former crofting townships to the crofters resulted in the continuation of poverty and overcrowding in the crofting communities. It also meant a continuation of protest by the landless families for land in the former crofting townships. By 1914 vast areas of land claimed by the landless crofters were used for sheep farms, deer parks and grouse moors.

Why did the land question become a problem again after the Great War?

When the war ended, many soldiers from the Highlands and Islands returned home with the firm belief that they had been promised land as a reward for fighting for their country. Propaganda, recruitment statements and speeches had made a firm link between Highland men and **their** land, and some large landowners did make promises of gifts of land from their own estates to men who had joined up to fight.

When the land the ex-soldiers expected was not given to them fast enough, many took the law into their own hands and began land raids.

What were land raids?

Land raids had been used in the 19th century when tempers ran high over the issues of clearances and absentee landlords exploiting the Highlands while the crofters starved. Land raids usually involved a number of men marching onto land they believed they should have a right to work on. Some claimed an old law stated that if they could build a wooden shelter and a hearth on which they could have a fire then they had a right to the land.

Did the Land Settlement Act of 1919 solve the problem?

The Land Settlement (Scotland) Act stated that land would be made available for men who had served in the war – but where would that land come from? For the Land Settlement Act to be successful the government would have to purchase land from the previous owners, but very soon it became clear the government could not afford to do so.

Land raids continued and the government was in a difficult position. It would be very expensive to meet the demands of all the ex-servicemen; to punish the land raiders would be very unpopular; to do nothing about land raiders would undermine the authority of the government.

To make matters worse, an official government report from the Board of Agriculture said that seizures of land would increase if the government's promises were not kept. By the end of the 1920s the problem of land ownership, overcrowding and poverty had still not been resolved in the Highlands. Many of the local people saw emigration as the only escape.

Was emigration a serious problem for Scotland in the 1920s?

In the inter-war period Scotland had the highest rate of emigration of any European country. In the 1920s emigration from Scotland became a flood. It was said at the time that Scotland was being emptied of its population, its spirit, its wealth, its industry and its talent. The 1920s saw an 'out migration' from Scotland higher than at any other time in Scotland's history. Many Scots saw emigration as an escape from a Scotland locked in unemployment and decline.

Did the Empire Settlement Act of 1922 boost emigration?

The Empire Settlement Act of 1922 provided for the first large-scale government-assisted migration programme. It was intended to boost the rural populations of Canada and other parts of the British Empire. Subsidies were paid to emigrants who agreed to work the land for a certain amount of time.

Emigration affected not only the Highlands. Lowland Scotland also saw the emigration of large numbers of skilled and talented labour. In the 1920s three out of ten migrants to New Zealand came from Scotland and the migrants were not only from the Highlands but also from the depressed industrial areas of central Scotland.

Emigration was also increased by the deliberate actions of the Canadian government in advertising their country. By the 1920s full-time resident agents encouraging emigration to Canada had offices in Glasgow and Inverness.

Issue 4 – How did the First World War affect Scottish politics?

This issue is about how the war made people think more about politics, how people became more political and what happened to the political parties.

To cover the syllabus you should know about the following:

- What radicalism is and how Scots were affected by it.
- What the ILP was and why many Scots supported it.
- What was meant by Red Clydeside.
- Why many Scots supported the union and wanted to be part of Scotland within Britain.

Radicalism and post-war Scottish politics

What were the main changes in Scottish politics caused by the war?

The Great War made many Scots more politically aware. A word used to describe that increasing awareness and willingness to become politically involved is 'radicalisation'.

The main changes in the political parties in Scotland involved the Liberals and the Labour Party. Before the war the Liberal Party was the most powerful political party in Scotland. After 1918 the Liberal Party was split and after the mid-1920s they would never again be such a significant force in British politics until the coalition government of 2010.

The Independent Labour Party was stronger in 1918 than it had been in 1914, and the mainstream Labour Party was about to become one of the two big parties in British politics.

The Conservative and Unionist Party recovered from their pre-war unpopularity and began to attract new voters from the middle classes living in the cities.

What does radicalisation mean and what effect did it have on post-war politics in Scotland?

To become politically radicalised means to want fundamental changes in the way politics operate. During the war, the radicalisation of politics in Scotland at times meant people taking direct action to cause or prevent changes to their own lives.

An example of this more direct action can be seen in the way that some women who became politically active in the rent strikes went on to become local councillors in Glasgow. In a similar way, the shop stewards of the Clyde Workers' Committee (CWS) went on to become MPs representing the ILP in the UK Parliament. Others became much more active in the trade union movement and in other campaigns such as anti-war groups in the 1920s.

The radicalisation of politics in Scotland greatly affected the main political parties. Many voters began to support the ILP or the Labour Party as a way of challenging the old ways of doing things. In that sense support for Labour could be seen as the radicalisation of Scottish politics.

The radicalisation of Scottish politics also had an effect on those who did not want change. Those people who were against the political changes supported by Labour also became stronger and more confrontational in their views. The Conservative and Unionist Party became the party of choice for many who saw it as the only way of stopping Scotland from sliding into 'Red revolution'.

The events of 'Red Clydeside' had given hope to people who wanted change in Scottish society but had also scared the middle and upper classes, who saw it as the possible start of revolution. In that sense Red Clydeside was a major cause of the radicalisation of Scottish politics.

Red Clydeside

What was Red Clydeside?

Between 1915 and 1919 parts of Glasgow and its surrounding area became known as 'Red Clydeside'. Red was the colour of revolution. The revolutionary flags flying during the Russian Revolution were all red so the nickname of 'red' for revolutionary stuck.

There were two phases to 'Red Clydeside'.

The first phase was a series of disputes in 1915 between the government and the workers in the factories and engineering works around the River Clyde. The second phase took place just after the war ended when strikes and conflict occurred between workers and police in George Square, Glasgow. This caused the government to worry that the strike leaders were preparing to start a revolution in Britain.

Why did the 'Red Clydeside' protests start?

Protests started in the engineering factories over the issue of dilution. You will remember that this meant the use in wartime of unskilled workers to do parts of a job that had previously been done only by skilled men. In other words, the skill was being lessened or diluted by the use of unskilled labour. Skilled men now saw their jobs under threat or, if they kept their jobs, it was certain their wages would be cut. If they complained they could be replaced by a group of quickly trained and low-paid women!

Why did tension increase between the government and the workers on Clydeside?

The government was worried when engineers at Fairfield's Shipbuilding and Engineering went on strike in February 1915. As the demand for munitions soared the government became very suspicious of any action by workers that might pose a threat to efficient wartime production.

Workers on Clydeside were angry with the Munitions Act. This new law made strikes illegal and also made any attempt to restrict or limit the production of war equipment and munitions a criminal offence.

Tension increased further when 'leaving certificates' were introduced. These new leaving certificates meant that workers now had to get permission to leave one job before they could get another, and the engineers felt this was another attempt to control not only what jobs they did but also where they worked.

The rent strikes were also part of the tension and discontent that rumbled through Clydeside in 1915. From the workers' point of view the rent strikes were successful. The government met the demands of the strikers and when the workers in munitions factories went on strike in support of the women organising the rent strikes, the striking men realised the power they had. They felt that any united action that threatened the flow of munitions would make the government sit up and take notice of strikers' demands.

The government took a different view. It was concerned about any attempt by workers to unite and perhaps disrupt wartime production. When the Clyde Workers' Committee (CWC) was started, its leaders Willie Gallacher and David Kirkwood, along with socialist John Maclean, soon became the centre of government suspicion. The CWC continued to organise small-scale strikes to protest at the removal of workers' rights. From the government's point of view, the CWC was a nest of revolutionaries ready to upset the war effort and even lead revolution in Britain.

What was the Clyde Workers' Committee (CWC)?

The Clyde Workers' Committee (CWC), led by chairman Willie Gallacher, was created to protect the interests of industrial workers. It was organised around shop stewards who were workers elected from the work place to represent the wishes of the workers themselves.

In January 1916, when the Dilution Commission arrived in Glasgow to enforce dilution in the munitions factories around Glasgow, the CWC led the workers in twenty-nine Clydeside engineering works. When strikes broke out, the government ordered the CWC leaders to be arrested and deported to Edinburgh, where they had to report to the police three times every day.

Did strikers on 'Red Clydeside' gain much public sympathy?

The deportations broke the strength and organisation of the CWC. Most public opinion supported the government. Newspapers described the strikers as being greedy and selfish. Most public opinion saw the strikers as damaging the chances of winning the war and even endangering the lives of soldiers at the front by trying to limit the supply of munitions. The letters pages of newspapers were full of demands that strikers should be put into the army!

Why did more 'Red Clydeside' protests break out at the end of the war?

When the war ended industrial workers across Britain began to fear for their jobs. They remembered the unemployment of the pre-war years and they realised that the war had given a temporary boost to industries that had been facing problems before the war. As munitions factories were closed, and orders from the government for the machines of war dried up, industrial workers also faced competition for jobs from thousands of returning soldiers.

On Clydeside the CWC was leading a campaign to reduce the working week of fifty-four hours to forty hours, partly to help create jobs for soldiers returning from the war. Prime Minister Lloyd George had promised returning troops 'a land fit for heroes'. Instead, most soldiers were disillusioned. There is a view that the Russian Revolution of late 1917 had inspired some workers to believe that great changes were possible. Faced with bad housing and unemployment in Scotland after the war, workers and soldiers alike wanted improvements in their living and working conditions.

The CWC held a meeting of its shop stewards in the shipbuilding and engineering industries in January 1919, where the Forty Hours Movement was established. The CWC promised that if there were still many people without a job even after a forty-hour week had been established then 'a more drastic reduction of hours will be demanded'.

What was the George Square Riot?

At the end of January 1919 the CWC and other trades unions called a strike and then a large demonstration in George Square, Glasgow for Friday, 31 January 1919.

As the crowds grew to almost 90 000 people the authorities became concerned and clashes between the police and protesters broke out. When the police launched a baton charge into the crowd, running battles between protestors and police spread across central Glasgow. The government had been advised that the crowd could easily become a revolutionary mob and the government's concern increased even more when some reports said a red flag was seen flying over the crowd. It was only fourteen months since the Russian Revolution, and in that same month of January 1919 a German Revolution had occurred. The government clearly felt it had to take action. Over 12 000 English troops were brought in by the government to restore order. Six tanks were also available for use and machine-gun posts were set up in the city.

Within a week of the battle of George Square, the strike was over and a settlement was reached on the basis of a forty-seven-hour working week. This was a victory for the workers in the short term but it did not seriously challenge the role of the bosses.

Was there really a risk of revolution starting on Clydeside?

There is little evidence that the leaders of the strikes and demonstrations ever considered challenging the authority of the British government. For most of the strikers and demonstrators the protests on Clydeside were the result of worries about dilution or unfair rents. At no point did most of the protestors think about revolution.

Did Red Clydeside have much effect on Scottish politics after the war?

Immediately after the events in George Square, membership of the ILP increased. The war, rent strikes and the image of 'Red Clydeside' seemed to have radicalised the voters in and around Glasgow.

Support for the Labour Party grew while the Liberal support fell. In 1922 several of the Red Clydesiders were elected as ILP Members of Parliament, including David Kirkwood and Emanuel Shinwell, both former leaders of the Clyde Workers' Committee, and also James Maxton and John Wheatley, leaders of the rent strikes of 1915–16. The success of the ILP in Glasgow gave rise to a real hope among the working people of Clydeside that gains could be made for Glasgow's working classes.

However, the hopes of the ILP members from Glasgow for real social change soon faded. The official Labour Party knew they needed middle-class votes if they were to be a national electable party, so they aimed at respectability and compromise. In effect, the Red Clydesiders were muzzled by a stronger and more moderate Labour Party, and were left largely without influence.

Political parties after the Great War

Why did the Labour Party become so important after 1918?

In the 1918 election the Labour Party gained one-third of all votes cast in Scotland. By the mid 1920s the Labour Party had replaced the Liberals as one of the two major political parties in Scotland. Some people might argue that the rise of Labour in Scotland had much to do with Red Clydeside, but there were several other reasons to explain the sudden rise of popularity of the Labour Party.

The Labour Party was helped by the Reform Act of 1918 that gave the right to vote to all men over twenty-one. Before 1918, the right to vote was linked to property ownership or a rental qualification so, by giving the vote to men on the basis of age almost inevitably the new voters would come from the poorer sections of society and would be more likely to vote for the working-class party representing their best interests – the Labour Party.

How important was the ILP to the success of Labour?

In Scotland membership of the ILP made up a third of all membership of the party in Britain. For many Scots in the 1920s, especially around Clydeside, the ILP **was** the Labour Party.

Some historians argue that the success of the Labour Party lay in the anti-war campaigns of the ILP, but that is far too simplistic. The argument also ignores the fact that the ILP's anti-war position was unpopular with the majority of Scots. Although the ILP was active in the anti-conscription movement and in opposing dilution of labour in the munition factories, the fact remains that the ILP was often seen as unpatriotic and damaging to the war effort. Out of nineteen ILP local councillors elected in the war years, only two were publicly anti-war.

What was attractive about the ILP was that their campaigns were very well organised and based closely on local issues that were important to the working classes of the area. Both the ILP and the Labour Party campaigned for reforms in housing and health after the war, and their focus on local issues was a big reason for Labour's success in the 1920s.

Were there other reasons for Labour success after the Great War?

In the west of Scotland the Catholic Irish vote deserted the Liberals and moved towards the Labour Party. Catholics were angered and offended by the way Lloyd George's Liberal coalition government had treated the Irish rebels after the Easter Rising of 1916.

Another reason why the Labour Party grew could be the extension of the franchise to women. In many of Scotland's cities working-class women had become politicised by their war work and the rent strikes. Women such as Mary Barbour, Agnes Dollan and Helen Crawfurd became role models for other women keen to make their voices heard politically for the first time.

Finally, a major reason for the rise of Labour was the parallel collapse of the Liberal Party.

Why did the Liberals lose so much support after the war?

Put simply, the war split the Liberal Party. From the very beginning of the war some Liberals supported the war effort while others opposed Britain's entry into the war. Some Liberals were founders of one of the main anti-war groups – the Union of Democratic Control. At the same, time the Liberal Party formed the government of Britain led by Prime Minister Asquith.

Arguments within the party weakened its organisation and demoralised party workers. Party funds collapsed as members stopped paying subscriptions.

Why did the Liberal Party split?

The Liberal Party had certain core beliefs at its heart. One of these was that the state – or government – should intervene as little as possible in people's everyday lives. Clearly, as the war dragged on the government became more and more involved in controlling what people could and could not do. Everything from DORA to conscription and on to rationing ran against the beliefs of old-fashioned Liberals.

The Liberal Party was also split by rivalry between Prime Minister Asquith and David Lloyd George, who eventually replaced Asquith as Prime Minister when the coalition government was formed in December 1916. Public opinion felt that Lloyd George would 'deliver the goods' whereas many felt that Asquith's slogan of 'business as usual' did not match the mood of a country involved in a world war.

The election that followed the end of the war marked the end of the Liberals as a united powerful party. The 'Coupon Election' of 1918 was so called because Liberal candidates who supported Lloyd George's coalition were given a letter of support from Lloyd George. The Liberals who supported Asquith referred to this letter as 'a coupon'.

The bitter contest between the two Liberal sections led soon afterwards to the decline of the Liberal Party as a major party in Scottish politics. By 1924 the Liberals had only eight MPs in Scotland and, when Asquith decided to give his support to the new minority Labour government, for many Scots the Liberals had simply ceased to matter. Scottish politics had become polarised between right and left wings. For Scots who feared the socialism of Labour there was only one answer – the Scottish Tories.

Why did the Scottish Conservative and Unionist Party gain support after the Great War?

To the government and a worried middle class the George Square riot provided proof that communist revolution was just around the corner. To the middle and upper classes it was clear that only the Scottish Tories could protect their interests. Before the war the Scottish Conservatives had gained most of their support from wealthy landowners and big businessmen. After the war a wave of middle-class city-based voters moved away from the Liberals and voted Tory. The Scottish establishment – the professions and the Church – gave their support to the Tories. Newspapers that had previously supported Liberal policies supported the Tories and by the early 1920s Scottish politics was a two-horse race between Labour and the Scottish Conservatives.

In summary, the Tories had not created new attractive policies. Their revival after the war was the result mainly of fear of Labour and the collapse of the Liberals as an effective counterweight to the threat of socialism.

Scotland after the war: a perspective

Although there will be no questions in the exam about this final section, it provides an opportunity to think about what the Great War meant to Scots and whether or not the war had any lasting effect on Scottish identity.

Before the war, most Scots were happy to be part of the union but the inter-war years were times of high unemployment and poverty and there were some Scots who believed that the union was no longer helping Scotland. Many Scots no longer saw England and the empire as being able to provide resources and leadership to overcome the economic and social problems affecting Scotland. Migration to England or the empire no longer promised a brighter future. Scotland was no longer the workshop of the empire. During the inter-war period, large-scale unemployment increased in traditional heavy industries such as shipbuilding, textiles and coal mining. Central government was blamed for doing very little. Nevertheless, most Scots did not question the place of Scotland within the UK.

A small group of Scottish nationalists did campaign for Scotland to be represented at the Treaty of Versailles to assert the principle of a small nation – but few Scots cared. In 1918, the Labour Party promised to fight for the 'Self-Determination of the Scottish People' but there was little public support. In the 1920s all three of the main political parties accepted without question that the United Kingdom would continue unchanged.

However, in the 1920s, economic distress did make more people interested in the possibility of independence. In May 1928, the National Party of Scotland was founded but it gained very few votes in the 1929 general election.

In the years after the Great War Scotland had to come to terms with the reality that had been growing before 1914. Scottish industry was in decline and only temporarily rescued by the boom years of the war. However, across the nation in towns and villages war memorials were built commemorating Scots who had died 'For King and Country'. For most Scots the king they had fought for was the king of Great Britain and the country they fought for was Britain. However, most of the Scots who had fought had done so wearing the kilt and hearing the sound of the pipes and drums. Politically, Scots accepted their part within the UK but, at the same time, their culture and identity remained Scottish.

Example question 1

Here is an example of a 'How useful…' question, linked to Issue 1 of the Impact of the Great War on Scotland. Remember that 'How useful…' questions can be used to assess **any** of the issues. Look back to page 5 and read what you have to do to answer a 'How useful…' type question.

Source A is from a letter written by Private Douglas Hepburn of the London Scottish regiment to his parents in October 1915.

> My dear mum and dad,
>
> We have been in the trenches for ten days and had a very rough time of it coming out with only 160 men left in our battalion. The Germans at the point where we attacked were ready and too strong for us. As we rushed up to the edge the machine-gun was turned on us and we suffered high casualties.
>
> Next day we could see all our dead bodies lying about in different positions, especially just in front of the Germans' barbed wire. To see thousands of our troops, stretching right across the plain to the horizon, and stretcher-bearers going here and there, doing their work and the wounded crying for the bearers. It was a sight that could not easily be forgotten. All I can say is that so far my luck has held up.
>
> Your loving son, Douglas

Question

How useful is source A as evidence of the experience of Scottish soldiers on the Western Front? (5 marks)

Writing your answer

Use the following advice to help write a fluent answer.

- *Paragraph 1*
  Write about the **origin** and **purpose** of the source. Why does the fact that it was written by a soldier from the trenches make it useful in terms of the question? Why do you think it was written (its purpose)? Why does the purpose help to make the source useful?
- *Paragraph 2*
  Refer to **one** point from the source and explain why it helps make the source useful. Develop the point made by using your own knowledge.
- *Paragraph 3*
  Refer to another point from the source and explain why it helps make the source useful. Develop the point made by using your own knowledge.
- *Paragraph 4*
  Finally, refer to a third piece of evidence from the source and explain why it helps make the source useful. Develop the point made by using your own knowledge.
- *Paragraph 5*
  Reach a final conclusion about how useful the source is. Mention the reasons that you think **do** make it useful, then include any reasons you can think of that might limit the usefulness of the source. What you have done is reach a **balanced conclusion**.

How many marks would you give?

- Is there a direct comment on how the **origin** and **purpose** of the source help to make it useful? You can get **up to** 2 marks for doing that.
- Are there three different points taken from the source? Are the points developed (explained) and is it clear why these points help to make the source useful? You can give **up to** 2 marks for doing that.
- Is there some recall used either to develop points in the source or used in the balance section to suggest the source is not as useful as it could be? You can give **up to** 2 marks for doing that.

Example question 2

Here is an example of a comparison question, linked to Issue 3 of the Impact of the Great War on Scotland. Remember that comparison questions can be used to assess **any** of the issues. Look back to page 6 and read what you have to do to answer a comparison question.

Source B is from Larry Marshall, a Scottish soldier whose family lived in Glasgow. He was interviewed in the 1970s when he was an old man.

> When I came back after the war my family told me how bad it had been. You see, us being an island hardly any food could get through, because German U-boats were sinking our food convoys. My family lived on bones from the butcher made into soups. And stale bread. When some food did get delivered to the shops everyone for miles around crowded round the place. The queues stretched for miles, and if you were old or unsteady on your feet you stood no chance. Many children died of starvation. Food riots were very common.

Source C is from the *War Memoirs* of Prime Minister David Lloyd George

> Our rationing system ensured a regular and sufficient food supply. It made it possible for those in charge to calculate with some precision how best they could make the stocks of available food-stuffs go round fairly. Although there was a degree of scarcity, we were never faced with famine or actual starvation. The steady improvement in our national health figures during and after the war shows that compulsory and careful control of eating was in general more beneficial than harmful in its effects.
>
> Thanks are due to our people for the patriotic manner in which they accepted these strange and unwelcome restrictions. Without general goodwill it would have been impossible to make rationing effective.

Question

To what extent do sources B and C agree about the supply of food during the Great War? (5 marks)

Compare the content overall and in detail.

Writing your answer

Use the following advice to help write a fluent answer.

- *Paragraph 1*
  Start by writing your overall comparison – do sources B and C agree or disagree about the effects of rationing?
- *Paragraphs 2–5*
  Deal with one detailed comparison in each paragraph. Find four points of comparison that the sources agree or disagree about. Explain each comparison fully by using brief quotes from the source and your own recalled knowledge.

How many marks would you give?

- Is there an overall comparison summing up the main difference between the sources?
- Apart from the overall comparison, are there four more direct comparisons made and is each comparison well explained and not just a series of quotes from the sources? If the answer is yes, then give 1 mark for each clear and correct comparison.

Top Tip

Usually in a comparison question you can gain marks for identifying and explaining points where the sources agree **and also** where they disagree. Don't always assume that the sources will take exactly opposite points of view. They might – but not always.

Example question 3

Here is an example of a 'How far...' question, linked to Issue 3 of the Impact of the Great War on Scotland. Remember that 'How far...' questions can be used to assess **any** of the issues. Look back to page 6 and read what you have to do to answer a 'How far...' type question.

Source D is from *Scottish Journey* (1935) by Edwin Muir.

> By the late 1920s the Clyde was launching merely 56,000 tons of shipping, and the coal industry was finding work for only 80,000 hands and producing a third less coal than in 1913. The Dundee jute trade was deeply depressed and the Borders woollen industry for the greater part of the year was on part-time working. The output of Scottish farming was falling while it was still rising in England, and in the fishing industry the numbers of those employed and the value of the catch were both steadily dropping.
>
> In the 1920s Scotland lost more of its population through migration than any other European country. From the Highlands and the Lowlands thousands of Scots realised that Scotland held no future for them and they set off for a better life in Canada or Australia where emigrant Scots might feel more 'at home'.

Question

How far does Source D give evidence of post-war economic change and difficulties facing the Scottish economy?

Use the source and recalled knowledge.

Writing your answer

Use the following advice to help write a fluent answer.

The source comments on examples of post-war economic change and difficulties such as: shipbuilding, coal mining, farming, fishing, the jute industry and migration.

Write a brief paragraph on each of these examples and try to outline (perhaps with quotes) the post war change and difficulties mentioned in the source.

You must then use your own knowledge first of all to develop and explain more fully the problems identified in the source. For example, you could write about the use of new fuel sources such as oil and foreign competition from abroad as reasons why the coal industry faced problems.

You should then use your own knowledge to write about other examples of post war economic change and difficulties not mentioned in the source.

How many marks would you give?

- Does the answer select information from the source and explain it briefly? You can give **up to** 4 marks for doing that.
- Does your answer provide a balance to the answer by using a lot of recall that is relevant to the question? You can give **up to** 7 marks for that.

Example question 4

Here is an example of a 'How fully...' question linked to Issue 4 of the Impact of the Great War on Scotland. Remember that 'How fully...' questions, like all the other question types, can be used to assess **any** of the issues. Look back to page 6 and read what you have to do to answer a 'How fully...' type question.

Source E is from 'Scottish Freedom', a magazine article written in 1918.

> Fellow workers, the country is at war. But does that mean we must lose our freedom? The Government and its supporters think that to get the best out of us, they must take away our liberty. We cannot work where we want to. We cannot leave without employer's permission and the government can even send us into the army to kill other working men from other countries just because they wear a uniform different to our own. Our socialist leaders are imprisoned and our women face persecution because they challenge the wartime profiteers and their rent rises. When we struggle for a 40-hour working week we are met with police charges and army guns.
>
> I say this – when we have a chance to vote again we must send men to Parliament – and women too – who will demand a change for the real people who are winning this war. The workers!

Question

How fully does Source E explain the impact of the war on political developments in Scotland?
Use the source and recalled knowledge.

Writing your answer

Use the following advice to help write a fluent answer.

The source refers to examples of how the war affected political developments in Scotland such as: increased government control over people's lives, conscription, rent protests and the campaign for a 40 hour working week. There is also a reference to voting for change at the next election.

Use your own knowledge first of all to develop and explain more fully the main issues identified in the source. For example, you could write about the rent strikes and the radicalisation of many women in Glasgow as an example of how the war affected political developments in Scotland.

Likewise, you could develop the references to the 40-hour week and its connection to Red Clydeside.

You should then use your own knowledge to write about other ways in which the war affected political developments in Scotland by using examples such as the decline of the Liberal Party.

How many marks would you give?

- Does the answer select information from the source and explain it briefly? You can give **up to** 4 marks for doing that.
- Does your answer provide a balance to the answer by using a lot of recall that is relevant to the question? You can give **up to** 7 marks for that.

When researching history topics for yourself, we recommend looking at the following websites:

- SCRAN (*www.scran.ac.uk*), a website run by the Royal Commission on the Ancient and Historical Monuments of Scotland, containing over 360,000 images and documents from museums and archives.
- Learning and Teaching Scotland's website (*www.ltscotland.org.uk/higherscottishhistory*), which has sections on all the units of Higher History.